the
DAL
COOKBOOK

the DAL COOKBOOK

Krishna Dutta

GRUB STREET · LONDON

Dedication

For my darling grandson Arun, who has been
nourished by my dal since he started life in his mummy's tummy

Published in 2013 by
Grub Street
4 Rainham Close, London SW11 6SS
email: food@grubstreet.co.uk
web: www.grubstreet.co.uk

Reprinted in 2014 (twice), 2015 (three times), 2016, 2017, 2018, 2019, 2021

Design and jacket design Sarah Driver
Photography Michelle Garrett
Food styling Jayne Cross

ISBN 978-1-909166-05-9
The moral right of the author has been asserted

A CIP catalogue entry for this book is available from the British Library.

Printed by Finidr, Czech Republic

Contents

INTRODUCTION

When I came to the UK as a young student from India in the late 1960s, British cuisine had a relatively poor reputation compared with that of other European countries such as France or Italy. What I ate then was often dull to say the least. Vegetables lacked variety, the range of spices was limited, and recipes in circulation were uninspiringly conventional. For me, food those days was merely fuel. I ate to live and to work.

Then one day walking down Drummond Street near University College London, I discovered a couple of small and shabby ethnic grocery shops selling exotic but well out of date vegetables like aubergine, mooli, stem of ginger and red chillies. I felt curious and walked in to find varieties of Indian dried lentils and pulses in packets on shelves. Promptly I bought a quantity of the ubiquitous red lentils and a few spices, a shrivelled piece of ginger and some dried chillies, went home and cooked them in the only pan I had on a small hob in our tiny bedsit with no fire escape. I can still recall the floating spicy aroma it generated and the thrill I felt savouring the dish with my husband and friends who happened to call in that day.

I did not soak the lentils before cooking, just threw in the spices I had bought and boiled them together. Nevertheless what I cooked instantly rejuvenated my Indian taste buds. I craved more. I also rediscovered the power of this simple staple dish I grew up with. In an instant I was liberated from the dreariness of the 60s British diet.

Later I began experimenting with other varieties available in those shops

with varying degrees of culinary success. At my request my mother sent me some of her recipes to try. I could not always get the spices she mentioned, so I began to recreate dal dishes with what was readily available. For example I garnished red lentils with fine fennel leaves from the back garden instead of coriander leaves as it was not readily available then and I dry-roasted split yellow moong lentils in the oven as the sun-dried variety was unobtainable.

As I continued to live and work in London cooking and serving lentils to family and friends, the dish of dal became a part of my set menu for suppers over thirty years. In fact it became my signature dish. During the 1980s and 90s my speciality in dal cooking earned some approval among British friends who tested my preparations and encouraged me to write down these recipes.

This prompted me to collect other Indian dal recipes and try them out in my kitchen. Soon I came to realise that dal is truly a pan-Indian dish consumed by rich and poor alike. I was most impressed by the multiple ways of cooking dal, the wide-ranging seasonings used and the diverse supplements to serve with it. I began to grasp how over the centuries Indian cooks became innovative. With locally available ingredients they dished out dal to satisfy a regional palate. In the process they also invented new dishes using dal lentils such as kedgeree (*khichuri* – a risotto made with dal), dosas (pancakes made with dal flour), vadas (dal fritters), dhokla (baked savoury dal cakes), poppadums (dal crackers) and pakoras (fried snacks dipped in

dal batter). The more recipes I garnered the more I felt the desire to share my findings with the food enthusiasts of my adopted country.

The nutritional content of this humble food also intrigued me. Dal is rich in protein and has practically no sugar and is known as 'poor man's meat' in India. Doctors now recommend it in a diet for diabetics. Indeed dal is so wholesome that it is one of the few dishes you could subsist on almost entirely and still be in good health.

Over the last two decades British food culture has been enriched by the impact of ethnic cuisine. Myriad spices, vegetables, lentils, pulses, beans and other ingredients are now widely available in restaurants and supermarkets. The word dal has now rightfully entered the British cookery lexicon. The time seems right to transfer my working notes on dal into a proper book for British gastronomes.

Krishna Dutta, 2013

WHAT IS DAL?

Etymologically the word has a Sanskrit origin meaning 'to split'. Applied to edible dried pulses, lentils and beans it came to suggest peas or beans, which have been stripped of their outer hulls and split. Later the word also came to denote the whole kernel with or without casing as well as the cooked dish.

In ancient Indian kitchens the word was transformed into a metonym and contemporary Indian restaurants often denote it as dal soup in the menu. However like most Anglo-Indian vocabulary the English spelling of this word is whimsical. The common variations are dahl, daal and dhal. Dal is more phonetic.

The Original Indian Staple

Archaeologists maintain that humans have been consuming lentils, peas and beans since the dawn of civilisation. A recent excavation on the border between Thailand and Burma carbon dated peas and pulses at around 9750BC. Crops have been cultivated in Central Asia, the Middle East and North Africa since antiquity.

Buddhism and Jainism, founded in India around 5th century BC, promoted vegetarianism, which prompted the search for protein other than meat.

Dal is mentioned in a Buddhist manuscript dated around the 10th century. One of the best records of Hindu courtly cuisine from the Chalukyan King Somesvara III (1126-1138) cites dal as an element

of a healthy diet. Ayurveda – the traditional Indian science of holistic wellbeing – highly recommends dal as a wholesome food and prescribes recipes.

Cheap to produce, highly nutritional, easy for long storage and able to be cooked with a basic pot on an open fire, this food has been providing quality nourishment to millions of impoverished Indians for millennia. The rich too customised its versatility to create sumptuous dishes fit for the Maharajas. Even the itinerant colonial officers on duty in distant parts of the subcontinents supped on kedgeree cooked by their Indian orderlies under open skies. Later the British expatriates imported this basic dish to Europe in its Anglo-Indian incarnation adding fish to the original vegetarian recipe. Supermarkets now mass-produce kedgeree as ready-made meals.

Though the affluent carnivorous communities in the west mostly neglected legumes except for a brief period of attention during the two world wars, British nutritionists and food connoisseurs have finally caught on to their value. More grocers, supermarkets and restaurants these days offer popular varieties of dal.

Historically the indigenous Hindu population were vegetarian and had been feasting on dal long before the Mughal invaders imported spicy curries to India from Persia to feed their carnivorous army.

The Indus Valley civilization is one of the world's oldest. It flourished during the 3rd and 2nd millennia BC and extended into north-western India. About 1500 BC Aryan tribes from the northwest infiltrated onto the Indian subcontinent and eventually merged with the earlier Dravidian inhabitants to create the classical Indian culture, which flourished until the 6th century AD when Islam spread across the subcontinent over a period of 700 years. In the 10th and 11th centuries, Turks and Afghans invaded India to establish the Delhi Sultanate. In the early 16th century European explorers established a foothold there. By the middle of the 19th century the British had colonised India and remained there till 1947. It is now an independent republic.

This bare outline of Indian history affirms the country's long exposure to foreign culinary influences through conquest and trade. Its climate ranging from tropical to temperate facilitates the cultivation of many wonderful herbs and spices. A blessed combination of these two factors may have contributed to the sophistication of India's cuisine. Possibly by virtue of this dynamic, the Indian cooks were able to turn apparently bland grains like pulses, lentils and beans into a mouth-watering meal of sustenance and satisfaction.

Thus classic dal cuisine is perhaps India's most original culinary gift to the world. I have long regarded dal as a life enhancing comfort dish. And I hope to help more people to discover this versatile and nourishing food for themselves.

TYPES OF DAL

The search for authentic recipes from various Indian regions also informed me that dal cooking varies distinctly from one part of India to another. Cooks prepare regional varieties altering the seasoning and spices as well as adding other ingredients such as meat, fish and vegetables. They may serve it as thick or runny, sour or sweet, savoury and full of flavour, and also as a hot soup or cool gazpacho. With a delicate nutty flavour, lentils, pulses and beans can easily blend well with accompaniments to make them delectable.

Although Canada is the largest grower of legumes, India produces by far the greatest variety – over 60 different kinds.

The most common Indian pulses and beans are:

KALA CHANA also known as chhole or Bengal gram. These are small brown or black skinned chickpeas. Tinned varieties are available.

GRAM DAL also known as **CHANA DAL**. These are the brownish yellow, hulled and split peas of **KALA CHANA** (Bengal gram). When ground it is besan or gram flour.

MASOOR DAL. A small brown, round, whole Indian lentil. The salmon-pink hulled and split variety, known as red lentils, is widely available.

MOONG DAL comes from whole, dark green, ovoid small moong (mung) beans. These can also be bought split and hulled either as green on one side and yellow on the other or both sides yellow.

TOOR, TOOVR or **ARHAR DAL**. These are round, hulled, yellow, split pigeon peas. There is an oily variety, which can be washed if preferred.

URID or **URAD DAL**. Black, ovoid, small, whole. available split and hulled with one side black and other side beige, or beige both sides (known as white lentils).

MATAR DAL. These are split from round medium sized matar peas and can be green, or yellow in which case they may be labelled yellow split peas. Green matar peas are also known as gunga or Congo peas and can now be purchased frozen, from some supermarkets.

KABULI CHANA. These are white chickpeas and are thought to have come from the Middle East via Kabul, Afghanistan. Also known as garbanzo beans.

GREEN or **BROWN LENTIL**. This flat, round, greenish brown, medium sized lentil, which originated in the West, is now popular in India.

RAJMA. Common red kidney beans.

The following tips may be useful for the storage and preparation of dal.

• Store in airtight containers at room temperature.

• Consume within six months of purchase – the older ones take longer to cook.

• You may need to pre-soak them in hot water for 30 minutes before cooking to restore moisture. Some use bicarbonate of soda to tenderise dals while boiling.

• Do not add salt, lemon juice or tomatoes before they are cooked to your liking. Acids make dal harder to soften.

• Pick out deceptive grits that maybe lurking before washing.

• Spices like cumin, black pepper, asafoetida and ginger help to digest dal.

• Beginners should start with common pink masoor dal known as red lentils.

General Guidelines for Cooking Dal

All dals need to be boiled until soft, with or without spices like ground turmeric, cumin etc. as required by the recipe and set aside before the 'tempering' treatment (see page 26). Different spices and other additions like meat and vegetables achieve variation in the taste of the cooked dal dishes.

Most dals bought from supermarkets can be cooked without any pre-soaking. Those that have languished for more than six months in your cupboard may need an hour's soaking in hot water before cooking.

Usually 250g lentils will require 700ml to 900ml of water to cook. You might need to experiment with this – the volume of water depends on the size and weight of your pan and whether you are cooking with gas or on an electric hob. Bear in mind that though dal is a forgiving dish and consistency can be a matter of taste, you can always try out various possibilities.

Some regular dal cooks use a pressure cooker to economise on time and fuel, others prefer to boil days ahead and divide into portions to bulk freeze.

Recipes in this book are authentic but can be adapted to suit you. Be imaginative. I have often reinvented traditional recipes to match my larder, my palate and my guest's predilections.

Do remember, Indian cooking is intuitive and improvised. None of the kitchens I visited even had a set of scales or a measuring jug. Recipes are handed down through generations and like Indian music, it is tricky to set them in western notation. It is sometimes difficult to be very precise with the use of standard measures in cooking Indian food, so measurements in all the recipes are a guideline. You might vary the amount of spices used according to personal preference and even introduce new ingredients and variations.

Be adventurous and try out new varieties. Know your favourites. Experiment with the cooking time. Keep a record. Learn from previous attempts. Be creative and explore possibilities. Create your own recipes and turn them into your very own signature dishes.

This is the joy of cooking dal. Its preparations have been endlessly recreated by millions of cooks through the millennia. I am hoping you will regard this book as an invitation to become a part of an extraordinary tradition of culinary ingenuity.

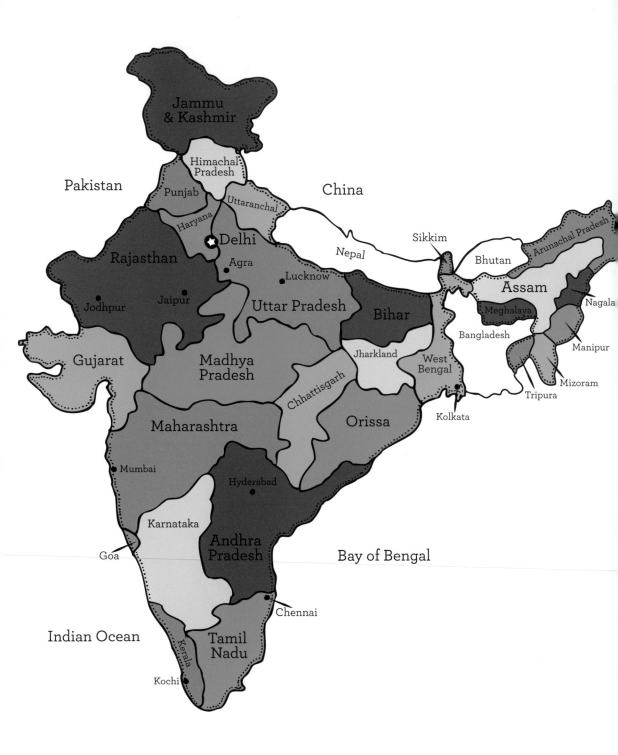

Jammu
& Kashmir

Himachal
Pradesh

Pakistan

China

Punjab

Uttaranchal

Haryana

Sikkim

Delhi

Nepal

Bhutan

Arunachal Pradesh

Rajasthan

Agra

Bhutan

Assam

Lucknow

Jaipur

Jodhpur

Uttar Pradesh

Bihar

Nagala

Meghalaya

Gujarat

Madhya
Pradesh

Jharkland

Bangladesh

Manipur

West
Bengal

Chhattisgarh

Mizoram

Orissa

Tripura

Maharashtra

Kolkata

Mumbai

Hyderabad

Karnataka

Andhra
Pradesh

Bay of Bengal

Goa

Indian Ocean

Chennai

Kerala

Tamil
Nadu

Kochi

NORTH-SOUTH-EAST-WEST

One can chart four distinct styles of dal cuisine through the four realms of India's North-South-East-West.

The variances in regional tastes are so ingrained in their palates that the same lentil may incite conflicting reactions from peoples of another province. For example, the north Indian cuisine is rich in spice, south Indians prefer sour tamarind and milky coconut in their preparation, east Indians like their food delicately flavoured and western Indians tend to use more chilli peppers to make it hot.

In addition to this broad simplification, some recipes combine meat with dal, others throw in prawns and fish. Vegetarians often add spinach, cauliflower or carrot and other vegetables. A characteristic local style is also vital to the authenticity of recipes: a key factor for the cohesion of a community. In a multi-faith society each religious group tends to observe their proscribed food restrictions. Therefore the cooks need to be creative and find alternative taste enhancing ingredients to avoid flouting cultural norm. For example, strict vegetarians adhere to spices like cumin or coriander instead of forbidden onion and garlic as these allegedly tend to induce passion.

'Unity in diversity' is the cornerstone of India's secular belief system. The culinary culture of India reflects this.

Economic disparity is another important factor in the choice of food preparation in the subcontinent. Thus a poor man may eat a simple meal of dal bhat (lentils with rice) whereas a rich man can afford a dish of saffron dal gosht (lentils with meat) with fragrant basmati rice or fried puri bread rich in ghee or clarified butter.

Furthermore as mentioned before, Indian food is highly influenced by the principles of Ayurveda – the science of life, compiled by two ancient physicians Charaka and Susruta, in the first century BC. As competent cooks, they classified food into categories and palates (*rasa*). According to them a healthy diet needs to achieve harmony with the local climate, seasonal variety of produce and individual vulnerability to sickness. They even prescribed and listed hot weather food to conserve energy and cold weather food to generate warmth. They instructed that palates such as hot, bitter, pungent, citric, salty should be regulated as they may induce thirst, sweat, bile inflammation and indigestion. Above all, food must be cooked to bring out its inherent therapeutic properties. It must be appetising, comforting and tasty. Indian cooks have almost always followed their Ayurvedic guidance.

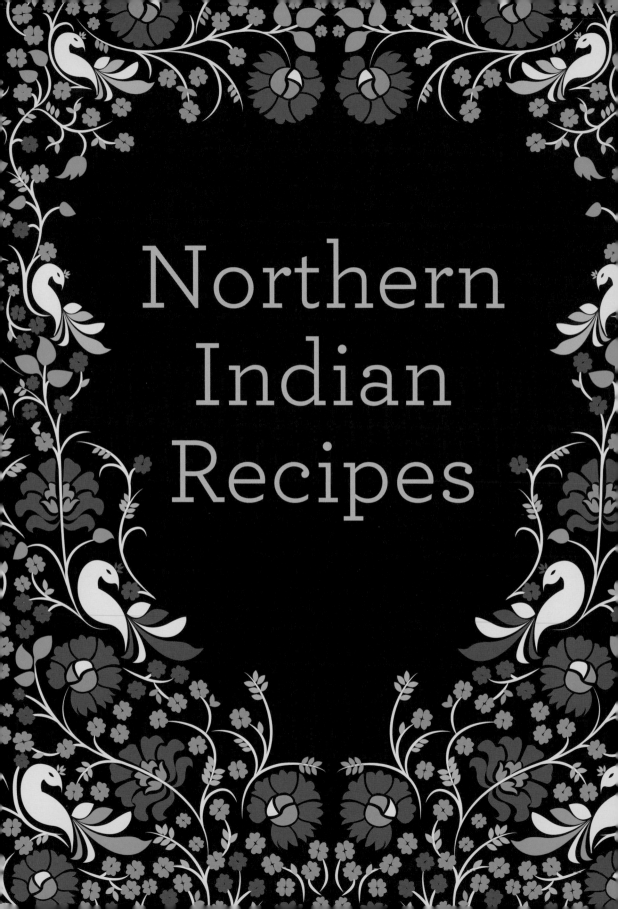

Northern Indian Recipes

Homemade in Uttar Pradesh

Dal Gosht

Tadka Dal

Punjabi Black Dal

Punjabi Nimbu Dal

Punjabi-style Dal Makhani

Dal Batti from Rajasthan

Dal Paneer Nawabi

Kashmiri-style Dal Makhani

Five Jewelled Dal from Chhatisgarh

Haryana Dal Maharani

Chicken Dal from Himachal Pradesh

Parsee Dal

Matar Peas and Paneer

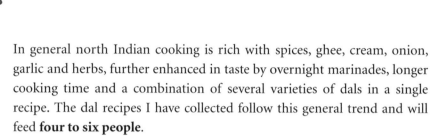

In general north Indian cooking is rich with spices, ghee, cream, onion, garlic and herbs, further enhanced in taste by overnight marinades, longer cooking time and a combination of several varieties of dals in a single recipe. The dal recipes I have collected follow this general trend and will feed **four to six people**.

Northern Indian states include Jammu and Kashmir, Himachal Pradesh, Punjab, Uttar Pradesh, and Kumayon among others.

The Tartar warlord Tamerlane ransacked Delhi in 1398 and since the 12th century, Muslims from Turkey, Persia and Afghanistan settled in north India. They lived alongside the indigenous Hindus in relative peace for some time until 1526 when Mughal Babur invaded Hindustan – the land of the Hindus. At the time consumption of meat was not in vogue among the Hindus on ethical as well as religious grounds; inspired by the Buddhist ideology, which had been promoted by the emperor Asoka (268-31BC), people lived mostly on a vegetarian diet. Mughals on the other hand were carnivorous people much used to mutton, beef and chicken. When they attempted to change the prevalent food cultures of their subjugated people, a skirmish between the two opposite culinary traditions erupted. Out of this initial conflict a kind of fusion cuisine slowly emerged and eventually Mughal gastronomy became synonymous with Indian cooking.

However each contemporary Indian state of north India with its distinctive use of spice and sense of taste continued to prepare the same dishes in slightly different ways. For example Dal Makhani – a rich spicy side dish manifested in two varieties, i.e. Kashmiri Dal Makhani and Punjabi Dal Makhani. The Kashmiri version uses more clarified butter and fresh herbs while in Punjab they tend to use cream and onions.

Homemade in Uttar Pradesh

The source of the sacred river Ganga (Ganges) lies here in Uttar Pradesh. It is also an important cultural region for Islamic Indians. Curiously most of India's prime ministers came from here.

This dal was cooked in Mathura by my host in a traditional kitchen with gleaming stainless steel pots and pans, jars full of spices and dals, and tins of rice and chapatti flour. I can still recall the spicy aroma of ghee and cumin.

150g split black urid dal
50g chana dal
2 tablespoons cooking oil
1 large onion, thinly sliced
ginger-garlic paste made from 2 cm fresh ginger and 4 cloves garlic
½ teaspoon ground turmeric
½ teaspoon red chilli powder
1 tablespoon ghee or clarified butter
1 teaspoon freshly roasted and ground coriander seeds
½ teaspoon garam masala mix (toasted and ground
cardamom, cinnamon and clove)
2 teaspoons fenugreek seeds (*methi*)
3-4 tomatoes, chopped

Soak the split black urid dal and the chana dal in hot water for 2-3 hours. Rinse them well and cook in approximately 700ml water until mushy. Set aside.

Sauté the sliced onion in a saucepan until it is soft and add ginger-garlic paste, turmeric and red chilli powder. Pour the boiled dals into the aromatic cooked spice mix. Add salt, to taste and a little water if required and cook for five more minutes. Take off the heat and set aside.

Heat the ghee in a frying pan and add ground coriander seeds, garam masala and fenugreek seeds and when it all begins to splutter, add the juicy chopped tomatoes and fry till soft. Now gently pour the cooked spiced sauce over the dal. Stir to blend and serve with chapatti bread or roti.

Dal Gosht

This dal is an example of early fusion cuisine. When in the sixteenth century, the Mughal's robust craving for beef and mutton clashed with the indigenous habit of eating lentils and legumes as a source of protein, the contemporary cooks may have inadvertently invented this rich and tasty dal of lentils and minced meat dish by way of gentle arbitration.

2 tablespoons cooking oil
1 large onion, peeled and chopped
3-4 crushed garlic cloves
500g whole masoor dal
6 small tomatoes, skinned and cut in halves
2 green chillies, seeded and sliced
thumb-sized piece fresh ginger, finely grated
500g minced lean beef or lamb
2 cinnamon sticks, 4 cloves and 2 whole
cardamom pods (garam masala)
1 teaspoon ghee

Heat the oil in a large saucepan over medium heat. Add the chopped onion. When the onion looks translucent, add the crushed garlic and toss a little to release the flavour. Put the dal into the pan with approximately 750ml of water, and cook for ten minutes. Watch so that it does not boil over, and skim off the scum if necessary. Add a little more water if required. Lower the heat. Add the halved tomatoes, sliced chillies and grated ginger. Add the meat stirring gently to mix well with the dal and cover the pan to cook slowly without losing much moisture and flavour. You may add a couple of cups of warm water in between if needed. Cook till the dal is mushy and the meat is tender. It may take 25 to 30 minutes to cook. The consistency needs to be just moist like thick gravy and not runny.

Take a small frying pan and dry fry the cinnamon sticks, cloves and the small cardamoms to release the aroma for a couple of minutes. Crush the dry fried spices in a pestle and mortar and immediately sprinkle over the cooked dish with a drizzle of ghee. Serve with chapatti or naan bread.

Tadka Dal

Indian cooking uses certain distinctive techniques such as Tadka. The word *Tadka* means tempering. It is done as a separate procedure by frying spices in hot oil to liberate the essential flavours from spice cells. Fried spices are then poured over the cooked dish. For tempering one needs to sense the right temperature of the oil so that the spices are not undercooked or over fried. The technique is to drop one spice seed in the hot oil and when it looks agitated, pour the rest in. To avoid burning always take the pan off the heat after briefly frying the spices.

150g whole urid dal (whole black lentils)
50g rajma (red kidney beans)
50g channa dal or yellow split peas
2 medium onions, chopped
2- 3 garlic cloves
thumb-size piece fresh ginger, peeled and sliced
2 green chillies
100g tomato paste or puree (I have also used fresh, finely chopped)
salt, to taste

For Tadka tempering
2 tablespoons cooking oil
2 teaspoons butter or ghee (clarified butter)
1 teaspoon whole cumin seeds
4 cardamom pods
4-5cm piece cinnamon stick
4 cloves
few peppercorns
1 teaspoon ground turmeric
1 teaspoon ground coriander
½ teaspoon fenugreek seed (*methi*) available
in some supermarkets

pinch asafoetida (*hing*) for authenticity
if you can obtain
2 tablespoons double cream (I have used
low fat natural yoghurt, beaten)
2 whole dried chillies

Soak all of the lentils (urad, rajma and channa dal) in warm water overnight, drain and then cover with 800-900ml of fresh water and slow cook in a pan on low flame till soft. It will take 2-3 hours. Set it aside.

Put chopped onions, garlic and sliced ginger with de-seeded chopped green chillies and tomato puree in a blender and reduce to a paste.

Choose a heavy saucepan and warm the 2 tablespoons of cooking oil in it. Add the 2 teaspoons of butter or ghee to the oil to melt. Gently fry cumin seeds and whole garam masala mix consisting of the cardamom pods, cinnamon stick, cloves and a few peppercorns. As the masala just begins to splutter, carefully pour in the blended ginger-garlic-chilli-tomato paste to calm it down. Stir the spice mix till golden brown. Now add one teaspoon each of the turmeric and coriander with fenugreek seeds and a pinch of asafoetida and fry. Add a little chilli powder for extra zing if preferred.

When the mixture begins to release the absorbed oil and the spicy aroma floats around, gently pour in the cooked lentils to the pan of the fried aromatic spice mixture. Bring it to a gentle simmer and stir for five more minutes. You may add a little water if it is too thick. The colour of the dish should be reddish brown now. Take it off the heat and gently pour in cream or beaten yoghurt and stir in. Put it aside for a couple of minutes and then warm over a low heat stirring lightly to release more flavour for another minute or so.

The rich dish is served usually with chapatti or naan bread. You can also freeze this and microwave later.

Punjabi Black Dal

This is a most simple recipe and can be prepared outdoors on a cooking pit with a few basic utensils such as a spoon, a bowl and a *karahi* – a kind of Indian wok with two handles. I have watched woodcutters and peasants preparing this for their midday meal of rotis, with ingredients brought from home, over a small earth oven full of smouldering twigs in a hurriedly dug hole.

500g whole masoor dal
thumb-sized piece fresh ginger, finely grated
2-3 cloves garlic, crushed
4 green chillies, seeded and sliced
2 tablespoons ghee
1 large onion, finely chopped
1 teaspoon ready-made ground garam masala
2 tablespoons single cream or beaten natural yoghurt
spring onions
salt, to taste

Cook the dal with grated ginger, crushed garlic cloves and sliced chillies in 800–900ml of water. Mash with a wooden spoon to a creamy consistency. Put aside.

Use a heavy frying pan, heat the ghee and fry the finely chopped onion till light brown. Add the ready-made powdered garam masala and gently fry to release the spicy flavour, which should take 20 seconds or so. Tip the fried onion and spice into the cooked mashed dal and stir in gently. Add a swirl of cream or yoghurt just before serving and garnish with chopped spring onions. Serve with warm rice. You can also have it with roti or parathas and meat or vegetable curry.

Punjabi Nimbu Dal

Nimbu means lemon in Hindi. This citrus fruit first grew in India and arrived in Europe via Italy during the Roman era. Ayurveda regards lemon as a valuable crop. Its sour quality prevents the excessive flow of bile and cleanses the mouth and the digestive tract. In the hot climate of India it is often used as a soothing drink and a preservative of food. This dal is a refreshing accompaniment with hot spicy dishes such as Mughlai chicken and mutton curry.

300g chana dal
1 lemon, cut in 2 halves
1 tablespoon ghee or clarified butter
2 cloves
2 cinnamon sticks
1 bay leaf
½ teaspoon cumin seeds
1 large onion, chopped
1 teaspoon ground turmeric
1 tablespoon fresh lemon juice
½ red onion, sliced
salt, to taste

Clean, wash and soak chana dal for one hour. Boil the dal in approximately 800ml of water, with one half of the lemon, till soft. Set aside.

Heat the ghee in a saucepan, add cloves, cinnamon sticks, bay leaf and cumin seeds and fry until they begin to splutter. Now add the onion to calm it down and fry together till brown. Add salt and the turmeric. Mix well. Tip the dal into the pan of tempered spices and let it boil for a few minutes. Add the fresh lemon juice, stir well and cover. Garnish with finely sliced lemon and sliced red onion. Serve hot with rice or chapatti.

Punjabi-style Dal Makhani

This classic dish is offered in Indian restaurants worldwide. Unlike the Kashmiri variety this can be cooked with three or four varieties of pulses, one of which is rajma (red kidney beans). Traditionally it was cooked on a low flame for many hours on a charcoal fire producing a thick mushy

consistency with a richly spiced flavour. Just before the end of cooking, a spoon of butter with a dollop of yoghurt was stirred in. But restaurants these days use pressure cookers for convenience and have altered the recipe to use a fair amount of thick cream to imitate the buttery taste.

50g rajma (small red kidney beans)
150g whole black urid dal
50g toor dal
50g whole green moong dal
small sprinkle chilli powder, to taste (optional)
50g melted ghee or clarified butter
2 medium onions, finely sliced
2-3 garlic cloves, crushed
thumb-sized piece fresh ginger, peeled and grated
2 green chillies
2 red dry chillies, cut into small slices
1 tablespoon ground cumin
100g chopped tomato (fresh or tinned)
100g butter
1 tablespoon whole garam masala consisting of: 2 sticks of cinnamon
some cloves and seeds from 1 large black cardamom pod
2 tablespoons double cream
salt, to taste

Soak the rajma beans overnight. Boil the dals in approximately 800ml of water with chilli powder (if using) till soft and set aside.

Pour the melted ghee in a heavy saucepan and sauté the onions till slightly brown. Add the crushed garlic and grated ginger to release the flavour. Swiftly add the green and red chopped chillies, cumin and chopped tomato to form a rough sauce. Watch the consistency of the sauce. It should not dry up. Slowly pour the cooked dals into the fried spices and stir in the butter. Leave it on a low heat for five minutes or so that the spices can blend well. Take it off the heat.

Take another small frying pan and toast the whole garam masala. Crush them using a pestle and mortar and immediately mix into the dals. Stir in the double cream and serve with fragrant pilau rice or roti.

Dal Batti from Rajasthan

This is a traditional recipe from Rajasthan. Originally started as an outdoor nomadic food cooked in an earth oven, it has now become a popular festive food for all occasions – religious and secular. This dish is usually served as a complete meal with a third component known as *Churma* or dessert, which I have excluded because most now prefer it without the sugary element. Compulsory in this recipe however is the five varieties of dals as the number five is auspicious for Hindus.

100g moong dal
100g urid dal
100g toor dal
100g channa dal
100g masoor dal
1 teaspoon ground turmeric
½ teaspoon chilli powder
3 tablespoons ghee or clarified butter
1 teaspoon cumin seeds
2 teaspoons fresh ginger, grated
¼ teaspoon asafoetida powder (*hing*)
2 green chillies, slit lengthwise
salt, to taste

For the Batti
300g whole wheat flour
150g coarse semolina
5 tablespoons gram flour (besan)
1 teaspoon salt
5 tablespoons ghee

Cook the dals till soft in approximately 800ml water with turmeric and chilli powder. When they are mushy and look like a thick soup, set aside.

Heat the 3 tablespoons of ghee in another saucepan and add the cumin seeds, grated ginger and asafoetida powder. Fry for two minutes to release the aroma and add the green chillies just before pouring the cooked dals into the pan and mix well. Add salt, to taste.

To make the Batti, put the flour, semolina, gram flour, salt and ghee into a large mixing bowl and mix well to make the dough. Knead the dough

for 5-7 minutes till firm. Set aside for 10 minutes.

Divide the dough into small balls and flatten them a little to make shapes resembling a £2 coin. Traditionally these are then baked in a clay oven but any oven will do. Lay them out on a lightly greased baking tray and bake for 20 minutes in a hot oven (180°C/350°F/gas 4) till medium brown. Brush them with a little ghee and dunk them into the cooked dal before serving in individual bowls or float them on the top of a large serving dish and let people eat from the common bowl.

Dal Paneer Nawabi

Paneer is an ancient form of fresh cheese made by adding lemon juice to hot milk; then discarding the curd and preserving the whey. It is widely used in Asian vegetarian cuisine as a good source of protein. Nawab is a Muslim honorific referring to Muslim rulers in northern India. But its British corruption nabob is usually a derogatory expression. However the juxtaposition of the two words refers to a rich dish fit for a Nawab!

200g pink masoor dal (red lentils)
100g rajma (try to use the Indian variety, which is smaller and tastier than the usual red kidney beans)
2 tablespoons ghee
1 large onion, sliced
2-3 garlic cloves, crushed
2 large tomatoes, skinned and sliced or chopped tinned tomatoes
½ teaspoon chilli powder
¼ teaspoon sugar
2 teaspoons tamarind paste, mixed in a small cup of hot water
thumb-sized piece fresh ginger, grated
4 green chillies, seeded and sliced
100g paneer or Indian cottage cheese (this is widely available in supermarkets)
2 tablespoons thick cream
handful coriander leaves, chopped
salt, to taste

Soak the kidney beans overnight or for 8 hours. Cook the dal and the rajma beans in approximately 800ml of water till mushy. Set aside.

Heat the ghee in a frying pan and fry the sliced onion till brownish, add crushed garlic to release flavour and chopped tomatoes until oily. Then add the chilli powder, sugar, tamarind water and salt. Fry together for a minute till spices blend and become piquant. Tip the contents into the boiled dal and put on to heat. Let it simmer. Now chop the block of paneer into small cubes and put them in a bowl of boiling water for five minutes to seal. Drain the water. Put them into the simmering dal and leave for a few more minutes. Remove pan from the heat and garnish with a swirl of cream and chopped coriander leaves. Serve hot with naan bread.

Kashmiri-style Dal Makhani

Makhani in Hindi means buttery. Before the arrival of the Muslim rulers in the fourteenth century, Kashmir was an important centre of Hinduism and Buddhism. On the whole, the food culture of the region reflects their adherence to vegetarianism. An eighty-year-old Kashmiri pious Hindu lady gave me the following recipe and said that she had never consumed garlic or onion, which are forbidden to devout Hindus. In her recipe, she used five varieties of dals as an auspicious combination.

50g urid dal
50g channa dal
50g masoor dal
50g toor dal (waxy variety)
100g moong dal
2 tablespoons ghee or clarified butter
1 teaspoon cumin seeds
¼ teaspoon Indian asafoetida (*hing,* if obtainable)
20g fresh ginger, julienned
1 tablespoon ground turmeric
1 teaspoon freshly ground homemade garam masala
consisting of 2 cinnamon sticks, 4 cloves and 2 whole
cardamom pods – dry roasted
1 teaspoon chilli powder
½ small pot (150g) natural yoghurt
1 tablespoon chopped coriander leaves
2 fresh chillies, slit lengthwise

Boil the dals in approximately 900ml water till soft, and set aside.

Use a large saucepan and warm the ghee till hot. Add the cumin seeds and the asafoetida. When they begin to splutter add the finely julienned ginger, turmeric, garam masala and chilli powder. Mix well. Watch the spices so they do not to burn. Now slowly pour the cooked dals into the saucepan of fried spices and bring to boil. Mix the yoghurt with a tablespoonful of water until it forms a smooth paste. Pour in and cook for a couple more minutes. Take off the heat and cool for 5 minutes. Stir in the chopped coriander leaves with the fresh chillies and cover the pan to retain the flavour of them and serve immediately with rotis or rice.

Five Jewelled Dal from Chhatisgarh

Chhatisgarh is the tenth largest state in India with a Chhatisgarhi dialect to reflect a distinct identity and culture, with the majority of the population being Hindu. It is primarily an agricultural area growing rice and pulses so people here consume dals in many forms such as poppadum and vadas. The name of the dish consisting of the auspicious five varieties of dals alludes to their faith though onions and garlic are often used in Chhatisgarhi cooking. I collected this recipe in Raipur, the capital of the state.

50g urid dal
50g channa dal
50g masoor dal
50g toor dal
50g moong dal
1 teaspoon ground turmeric
½ teaspoon chilli powder
1 teaspoon ground garam masala
2 large onions, chopped finely
2 tablespoons ghee
1 teaspoon whole cumin seeds
½ teaspoon whole coriander seeds
1 tablespoon freshly grated ginger
2-3 garlic cloves, crushed
juice from one lemon
2 tablespoons natural yoghurt
handful of chopped mint

Boil the dals in approximately 800ml water with turmeric, chilli powder, garam masala powder and chopped onions till soft. Do not skim off the scum. Set aside when cooked into a mush.

Take a large frying pan and pour in ghee to melt. Add the cumin and coriander seeds with the grated ginger. As they begin to splutter add the crushed garlic to release flavour. Immediately and carefully toss the mixture into the pan of cooked dals and bring it back to the heat. Simmer for 3-4 minutes then take it off the cooker. Squeeze in the juice from one lemon and garnish with a dollop of yoghurt and chopped mint leaves and serve with roti, paratha or pilau rice.

Haryana Dal Maharani

Haryana is one of the most economically developed states of India and a major hub for information technology. Part of this state was the home of the ancient Indus Valley civilisation. Despite industrial development, it retains a large agricultural sector growing varieties of pulses and lentils with other crops and a strong tradition of dairy farming. The Haryana government provides free education for women up to the Bachelor's Degree level. Perhaps naming the recipe as maharani and not maharaja is an example of their awareness of gender equality.

250g toor dal
thumb-sized piece ginger, peeled and grated
3 garlic cloves, crushed
2 tablespoons melted ghee or butter
2 onions, peeled and chopped finely
½ teaspoon Indian asafoetida powder (*hing*)
3 tomatoes, skinned and chopped
1 teaspoon chilli powder
1 teaspoon ground turmeric
2 tablespoons beaten natural yoghurt mixed with ½ teaspoon jaggery
or brown sugar
2 green chillies, seeded and sliced
2 red chillies, seeded and sliced

Place the dal in a saucepan with approximately 700ml water, bring to the boil and skim off any scum and froth that rises to the surface of the liquid. Reduce the heat, partially cover the pan and simmer for 25-30 minutes until the dal is soft and has broken down. Chop the ginger and garlic into a rough paste. Heat the ghee or butter in a saucepan; add the onions and fry for 6-8 minutes, stirring occasionally, until lightly browned and add asafoetida. Next turn the heat down to add the garlic and ginger paste, tomatoes, chilli powder and turmeric to the pan and fry gently till aromatic and oily. After 2-3 minutes of gentle frying, tip the cooked lentils into the saucepan of aromatic spices, season well with salt and leave to simmer for 8-10 minutes until thick. Stir through the yoghurt blended with a little sugar. Use a whisk. Garnish with deseeded and sliced red and green chillies floating on top. Serve with chapatti or puri bread.

Chicken Dal from Himachal Pradesh

Located in the heart of the western Himalayas, Himachal Pradesh is a spectacularly beautiful Indian state of great natural attraction where the Dalai Lama resides. Although not a distinctive culinary region, I have included this because it comes from the little known tribes of mountain people – the *Paharis*. Until recently they had a very limited supply of fresh vegetables and relied on potatoes and onions for much of their cooking.

1 whole chicken, cut into small pieces
1 small pot (150g) natural yoghurt
juice of one lime
2 teaspoons ground turmeric
2 dried chillies, crushed
2 teaspoons ground cumin
2 teaspoons ground coriander
2 tablespoons melted ghee
2 onions, peeled and finely chopped
3 garlic cloves, crushed
250g channa dal
250g green lentils
thumb-sized piece ginger, peeled and grated
2 bay leaves
4 cardamom pods
1 small cinnamon stick, split
6 cloves

Marinade the pieces of chicken with approximately 100g of the yoghurt and lime juice, with one teaspoon each of turmeric, chilli, cumin, and coriander overnight.

Put one and half tablespoons of melted ghee in a large heavy saucepan and sauté the onions till soft. Add the crushed garlic. When you smell the garlic add the dal and lentils and ginger and toss around for 20 seconds. Pour in 500ml warm water and let it boil with the remaining one teaspoon each of powdered turmeric, chilli, cumin, and coriander. Turn the heat down and add the marinated chicken pieces. Add the bay leaves, cover the pan, and let it cook slowly for approximately an hour. Add more water gradually to avoid it drying up. When the dals are soft and the chicken is cooked, stir in the rest of the yoghurt and blend well. Take it off the heat.

Add salt, to taste.

Next toast (dry fry in a frying pan) the cardamom pods, cinnamon stick and cloves and crush them in a pestle and mortar. Sprinkle them over the freshly cooked chicken. Drizzle over the rest of the melted ghee. The dish should be gooey. Serve with parathas, naan bread or rice and some lime pickle.

Parsee Dal

The Parsees sailed from the Gulf to Gujarat fleeing a religious persecution around 1100AD and enriched the Indian culinary culture in many ways particularly through the use of saffron in cooking rice and adding a 'pinch of sugar' in spicy dishes. The celebrated dish 'Dhansak' is an example of their influence. This recipe displays an interesting interplay of flavours and taste.

500g salmon-pink masoor dal (red lentils)
1 teaspoon chilli powder
1 teaspoon brown sugar
1 teaspoon ground black cardamom
1 teaspoon ground cloves
½ teaspoon coarsely ground black pepper
pinch saffron strands
25g butter
2 large onions, peeled and finely chopped
4 garlic cloves, finely crushed
2 green chillies, deseeded and sliced
salt, to taste

Boil the dal with the chilli and brown sugar. When soft and dense take it off the heat and stir in the ground cardamom, cloves and black pepper and the saffron strands. Mash the contents with a wooden spoon. This will bring out the flavour of the ground spices and the saffron. Set it aside for five minutes.

In another saucepan melt the butter slowly and sauté the onions till translucent then add the garlic. As the aroma rises, stir the spiced and mushed dal into it and blend well and add salt, to taste. Take it off the cooker and sprinkle the sliced chillies on top. Serve this warm fragrant dish with roasted or barbecued meat and naan bread.

Matar Peas and Paneer

Fresh shelled green peas and paneer make a nutritionally winning match but as peas are a seasonal crop, inventive Indian cooks came up with this variation that can be prepared year round. Matar peas, though authentic, may not be easily available, so use kala channa available in tins. I have also cooked this with 400g of frozen green peas as well as with tinned chickpeas.

500g dried matar peas (soaked and cooked beforehand)
250g paneer block, cut into small cubes
2 tablespoons melted ghee
2 large onions, peeled and finely chopped
3 garlic cloves, crushed
thumb-sized piece ginger, peeled and grated
1 teaspoon ground turmeric
1 teaspoon chilli powder
2 teaspoons ground coriander
1 tablespoon ground garam masala
3 or 4 tomatoes, skinned and chopped
2 tablespoons double cream or yoghurt
2 green chillies, seeded and sliced
1 tablespoon chopped spring onions
½ green lime, thinly sliced

Start the night before by soaking the dried matar peas if using. Then boil peas in sufficient water to cover, until they are soft.

Fry the cubes of paneer in the melted ghee till golden. Paneer emits fat so the cubes will turn golden in approximately 30 seconds (and you will have more fat than what you started with). Take them out and set aside. Toss the onions, crushed garlic and grated ginger in the same pan. Cook slowly on a low heat till onions are soft. Add turmeric, chilli, and coriander with the garam masala and fry them till the oil separates from the spice mixture and the aroma rises. Tip the cooked matar peas (tinned kala chana or chickpeas or frozen peas) into the aromatic pan. Stir in the chopped tomatoes. Add a little water if required and salt, to taste. As it begins to simmer slowly, put the fried paneer pieces back in the pan and leave it for a couple of minutes. Stir in the cream or yoghurt gently and sprinkle with the green chillies, spring onions and lime slices on the top before serving.

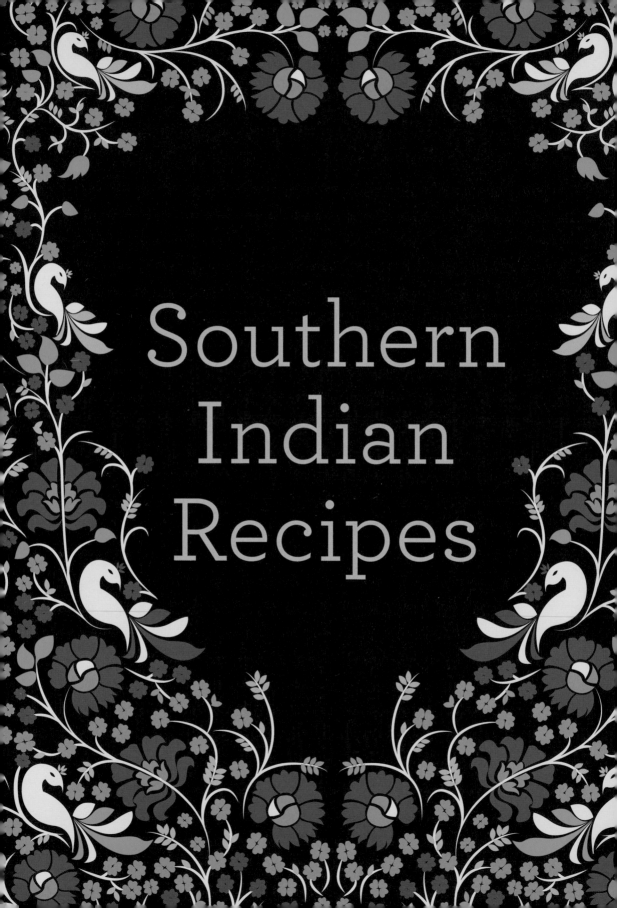

Southern Indian Recipes

Rasam with Gourd and Toor Lentils

Sambar

Onion Sambar

Ginger Rasam from Kerala

Lentil Kutu with Green Beans

Coconut Gram Dal

Mixed Vegetable Sambar Stew
from Tamil Nadu

Paruppu Thogayal

Dal Vadas

Olan with Pumpkin from Kerala

Plain or Stuffed Dosas

Idli

Shahjahani Dal from Hyderabad

Tamil Toor Dal with Okra

The southern coastline of India was once the most important trading shore in the ancient world serving as a link between the Far East and the West. India's contact with the Mediterranean peoples such as the Phoenicians, Romans, Greeks, Arabs and Syrians among others, began here.

Over a long period of time, several significant Indian dynasties like the Cholas and the Pallavas ruled this area and encouraged the growth of the distinctive literary, artistic and architectural culture of Southern India. However in the late medieval period it fell into the hands of the Muslim rulers and a large Muslim community still inhabits the coast of Malabar.

Judaism arrived in Kerala 2500 years ago and later the Jews became a key player to mediate between the Indians and the western traders. St Thomas the Apostle is believed to have arrived there too in 52AD and founded the Syrian Christian tradition. Christianity has flourished in the region ever since.

The French colonial architecture lining the grid pattern streets, and a small French speaking population at Pondicherry (*Puducherry*) tells you that it was once a French enclave (till 1954).

Because of the convergence of all these different communities, a distinctive food culture has taken root here.

Fish and coconuts are common ingredients of the coastal South Indian kitchen. However this is a big region, and it is home to distinct communities, so while there is some common ground, there are also sub-sectional

variations and traits. For example, Andhra Pradesh cuisine is often hot and spicier while the Nizami tradition in Hyderabad is rich with butter and cream similar to the Mughal tradition.

Dried or fresh curry leaves are used in almost all dishes in Tamil Nadu and Kerala for flavouring the recipes. They are now widely available in supermarkets. Unlike other parts of India, southern cooks often use freshly ground dals instead of the whole kernels and the South Indian dals are often runnier – more like a soup than a stew.

The dal dishes I have collected are mostly from domestic cooks who have had family recipes passed down through generations. South India is truly a paradise for vegetarians. Recipes are simple and can sometimes be sweetened and soured with the use of homemade yoghurt or tamarind juice. Some also use kokum – a native fruit. This fruit has no English name, because it is indigenous to India and is rarely seen outside the Konkan region and some parts of Gujarat. The purple kokum fruit contains eight seeds and grows on a slender evergreen tree. This sweet and sour fruit is picked and the rind removed, then soaked in the juice of its own pulp and dried in the sun. The rind is used as a flavouring agent and can also be soaked in water to make a refreshingly cool summer drink. Kokum seems to enhance the taste of coconut, which makes it particularly effective in these dishes. However I have left this ingredient out as it is almost impossible to find outside its native region.

Rasam with Gourd and Toor Lentils

Rasam means juice in Sanskrit. It can be made using tamarind, lemon, ginger, garlic or pepper as a basic ingredient. The tamarind rasam is the most common one.

The Indian gourds can be bottle shaped or spherical with easy to pierce smooth green rind. They grow profusely and can be ground spread as well as climbers. This refreshing dish is usually served as a starter or a side dish often with a dollop of warmed fragrant ghee, with a main meal of rice, dosa (the traditional thin pancakes made from rice flour), and idli (rice and urid dal steamed cake).

2 tablespoons coconut oil or sesame oil
1 teaspoon whole mustard seeds
1 onion, thinly sliced
thumb-sized piece root ginger, finely pulverized to
make a paste
2 garlic cloves, finely crushed
¼ teaspoon ground turmeric
¼ teaspoon red chilli powder
250g toor dal
200g gourd (or any squash), cut into small cubes
1 tablespoon tamarind puree
10-12 curry leaves, fresh or dried
1 teaspoon dried crushed red chilli (optional)
salt, to taste

Heat the oil in a pan and when hot, throw in the mustard seeds. A few seconds later, add the sliced onion, ginger paste, crushed garlic, turmeric and chilli powder. When they become creamy and translucent, add the dal with 500ml of water. Bring to the boil and then simmer until the dal is cooked. Now stir in the cubed gourd and the tamarind puree and simmer it till cooked. It should take five to ten minutes. Add the curry leaves, and the dried crushed chilli (if using) near the end of cooking time, cover the pan and take it off the heat. The consistency should be on the thick side like a tin of baked beans. Serve hot with freshly cooked rice.

Sambar

Sambar is a standard watery South Indian dal dish. It usually contains local vegetables like okra or aubergine cut into small pieces. I have also had potato and carrot sambar. The other essential ingredients are tamarind and dried red chillies.

1 tablespoon coconut oil or sesame oil
1 teaspoon mustard seeds
1 onion, thinly sliced
2 garlic cloves, crushed
thumb-size piece root ginger, finely grated
½ teaspoon each cumin seeds and coriander seeds, roughly pounded
2–3 dried red chillies
200g split toor dal
50g ground gram dal
50g whole urid dal
¼ teaspoon ground turmeric
¼ teaspoon red chilli powder
1 tablespoon seedless tamarind paste
¼ teaspoon dried ground fenugreek seeds (*methi*)
1 small potato, cut into bite-sized pieces
1 large carrot, cut into bite-sized pieces
100ml coconut milk
salt, to taste

Heat the oil in a saucepan and when hot, throw in the mustard seeds. As it splutters, add the sliced onion with the crushed garlic, grated ginger, the pounded cumin and coriander seeds and the dried chillies. When the onion becomes translucent, add all the dal, turmeric, chilli powder and tamarind paste and fry with the fenugreek seeds for two more minutes. Slowly pour over 700 ml water. Bring to the boil then simmer until the dal is almost cooked. Now add the potatoes and carrots, and cook till soft. Stir in the salt and coconut milk near the end of the cooking time and cover the pot. This is a watery dish so add more water if required. Turn off the heat. Leave aside for a couple of minutes before serving this dish warm with boiled rice and sour pickles or as accompaniment to dosa or idli.

Onion Sambar

225g ground green moong dal
2 teaspoons coriander seeds
40g ground gram dal or besan
pinch asafoetida powder (hing, if available)
1 teaspoon fenugreek seeds (*methi*)
2 teaspoons grated coconut
10 small pickling onions, peeled
1 teaspoon ground turmeric
2 teaspoons thick tamarind paste
5–6 curry leaves
1 teaspoon vegetable oil
½ teaspoon mustard seeds
salt, to taste
2 tablespoons chopped, fresh coriander leaves
½ teaspoon chilli powder

Start by grinding the whole green moong dal in a food processor. Dry fry the coriander seeds, ground moong dal, gram, asafoetida and fenugreek seeds together for the aroma to be released. Leave to cool and grind them together. Add the grated coconut to the mixture.

In a saucepan boil the peeled onions for three to four minutes with turmeric and salt. Add tamarind paste to the pan. Now add the fried ground spice and dal paste to the cooked onions. Add more water as this is a fairly runny dish. Crush and add the curry leaves, cover and take off the heat. In a small pan heat the oil and throw in the mustard seeds until they splutter. As soon as they do pour them into the cooked dal mixture, add some salt to taste and garnish with chopped coriander leaves and a sprinkle of chilli powder. Serve with plain rice.

Ginger Rasam from Kerala

The finest ginger comes from Kerala. It is a rhizome (a kind of root) that grows quite a size underground. Root ginger has been used as a medicine and as a flavouring delicacy in India from ancient times. It came to the west via the Silk Route. I had this dish at the famous old colonial Madras club in Chennai. When the cook saw I was suffering from a cold, he served me this to clear my head. I loved its taste and smell so much that I managed to prise the recipe from him.

150g toor dal
¼ teaspoon ground turmeric
¼ teaspoon red chilli powder
2 tablespoons vegetable oil
1 tablespoon coconut oil
½ teaspoon cumin seeds
2 teaspoons freshly grated ginger
2 teaspoons tamarind paste
½ teaspoon mustard seeds
4-5 fresh or dry curry leaves
¼ teaspoon fenugreek seeds (*methi*)
1 tablespoon chopped coriander leaves
2 fresh green chillies, deseeded and sliced
salt, to taste

Boil the dal in 750ml of water with the turmeric and chilli till soft and set aside. Mix the vegetable oil and coconut oil together, and fry the cumin seeds in approximately two tablespoons of the mixed oil in a frying pan and when cool roughly grind them to make a paste. Add this to the cooked dal. Mix the freshly grated ginger and tamarind paste together in a cup of warm water and add to the pan of dal. Put the saucepan of cooked dal back on the heat and allow this to simmer for a few minutes. Add more water if required, as this dish is usually served runny like milk. Now take the frying pan used before and fry the mustard seeds in the remaining tablespoon of oil. When they start popping, add the curry leaves and the fenugreek seeds. Toss them about a little. Pour this seasoning over the simmering dal. Garnish with chopped coriander leaves and sliced green chillies. Serve the refreshing rasam just as a consommé soup or with some boiled rice in a bowl.

Lentil Kutu with Green Beans

Kutu is a dry vegetable dish usually cooked without any oil or butter. This pappy dish is usually made with greens beans but other vegetables can be used. Like Olan (page 60) this traditional simple dish is refreshing and nourishing. It is popular among the rich and the poor alike. Some people add a dollop of aromatic melted ghee just before serving the dish. I have enjoyed it for lunch, served simply with a slice of lemon at a cheap roadside eatery.

250g moong dal
500g small sliced green beans
½ teaspoon ground turmeric
½ teaspoon mustard seeds
1 tablespoon coriander seeds
1 teaspoon rice
½ fresh coconut, grated or 200g grated
from a creamed block or desiccated soaked in milk
small pinch asafoetida powder (*hing*)
1-2 dried red chillies, roughly crushed
salt, to taste

Boil the dal in 600-700ml of water, adding more water frequently as it evaporates and strain all the liquid when cooked. Save about two cups of the same liquid in a pan, enough to cook the beans in. Now cook the green beans briskly with the turmeric till tender in the saved dal liquid.

Grind all the spices – mustard seeds, coriander seeds and the rice and make a paste with little warm water. Tip the cooked lentils and the spice paste into the pot of cooked green beans, along with the coconut. If using fresh grated coconut you can reserve a little for garnish. Add a pinch of asafoetida powder, crushed chillies, salt and a little more water if required. This dish ought to have a sticky consistency. Just before serving you can garnish with some freshly grated coconut. Serve with boiled rice.

Coconut Gram Dal

Bengal gram, also known as kala channa or *chhole*, is widely grown in India. They are black and smaller than chickpeas. In the west it is sometimes recommended to people with diabetes as it is nutritious and has a low glycaemic index. This recipe was given to me by a cook in Trivandrum.

250g kala chana
½ tablespoon urid dal
2 tablespoons sesame oil or an equal mixture of
coconut and vegetable oil
Thumb-size piece root ginger, finely grated
1 tablespoon sliced spring onion
½ teaspoon mustard seeds
2 dry red chillies, seeded and sliced
100g freshly grated coconut, or grated from a creamed
block or desiccated soaked in a tablespoon of milk
2 tablespoons coconut milk (tinned)
1 lime, to serve
1 green chilli, to serve
salt, to taste

Boil the two dals together in 700ml of water till soft, and set aside. The small measure of urid dal is used in this recipe to make it a little creamy.

Pour the oil into a large saucepan and briskly fry the grated ginger and the spring onion. Do not over fry them – the aim is simply to enhance flavours. Now in the same hot oil add the mustard seeds and as they begin to splutter add the chopped chillies and toss about. Beware, the fumes of over fried chillies might tickle your throat. Before that happens, tip the cooked dals into the saucepan. Stir the contents in with a whisk and bring them to simmer. After five minutes or so stir in the freshly grated coconut and take it off the heat. Pour in the coconut milk and blend well. Let it rest for another minute then serve over a bowl of boiled rice and a slice of lime with a raw green chilli on the side. Some might like to take intermittent bites into the fresh chilli like the locals.

Mixed Vegetable Sambar Stew from Tamil Nadu

This dish was cooked at my host's home and then carried by her family to an enchanting picnic spot by the waterfalls of Ernakulam. After a long drive we had it for lunch served over some freshly boiled rice cooked over a pit fire. The meal was laid out on a washed, rectangular, plate-sized piece of green banana leaf. We ate with our fingers and licked them clean. Eating this dish at home in London always takes me back to that magical day.

200g toor dal
50g channa dal
50g urid dal
2 large tomatoes, peeled and chopped
6 shallots, sliced
1 whole aubergine, cubed
1 large potato, cubed
1 small gourd or pumpkin, cubed
100g okra, in bite-sized pieces
1 teaspoon ground turmeric
1 tablespoon pulped tamarind or tamarind paste mixed
with warm water
1 tablespoon sesame oil or an equal mixture of
vegetable and coconut oil
1 teaspoon mustard seeds
5-6 curry leaves
½ teaspoon ground asafoetida (*hing*)
2.5cm cube palm jaggery (available in Asian grocers) or 2 teaspoons
brown sugar

For seasoning
1 tablespoon coriander seeds, dry roasted in a pan and ground
1 teaspoon cumin seeds, dry roasted in a pan and ground
2 tablespoons freshly ground coconut or desiccated soaked in milk
One dried red chilli crushed roughly or ½ teaspoon chilli powder

Boil the dals in a heavy saucepan in 600-700ml water. When cooked add all the vegetables to the pan with the turmeric and cook for 7-10 minutes or till

soft. While the vegetables are cooking prepare the seasoning. Then stir in the roasted and ground seasoning, tamarind liquid, and salt. Add a little water if the mixture appears too thick.

Put the sesame oil into a frying pan and when hot add the mustard seeds, the curry leaves and asafoetida. As they begin to crackle stir in the palm jaggery and let it melt into it. Now tip the contents of the frying pan into the saucepan of the cooked dals and the vegetables. Simmer it for two minutes and serve with rice.

Paruppu Thogayal

In Tamil *paruppu* means lentils or dal and *thogayal* is pickle or chutney. I had this accompanying dish with a dosa in Kerala. It can also be eaten with idli (steamed rice cake). It is a dry and spicy kind of dal relish, really a kind of Indian lentil dip.

1 tablespoon coconut oil
250g toor dal
125g grated fresh coconut or creamed
3 garlic cloves, finely chopped
pinch asafoetida powder (*hing*)
2 dried red chillies, crushed
1 tablespoon tamarind paste
1 tablespoon finely chopped mixed mint and coriander leaves
salt, to taste

Heat the coconut oil in a pan and fry the dal, coconut and garlic for a couple of minutes and add the pinch of asafoetida. Take it off the heat and soak the mixture in approximately 250ml warm water with the crushed chillies for an hour. Then grind it to a rough paste. If you prefer a smoother *paruppu thogayal*, add a little more water and leave for another forty minutes before soaking and grinding again to attain a creamy texture. Now stand the mixture in a warm place for a couple of hours to ferment. Add the tamarind paste with the chopped mint and coriander leaves and blend well. Then serve as a dip with dosa or idli or eat with boiled rice, rasam and poppadum.

Dal Vadas

South Indian vadas are spicy and crunchy deep fried lentil balls or fritters. Like the onion bhaji or samosa, vadas are usually eaten as a warm snack. Ancient in origin they can be quickly prepared even at a roadside with just a small stove and a bowl of batter, which is why vadas have been one of the most enduring and popular street foods in India.

You can get the dal vada mixes in packets with easy to follow instructions from Asian food shops but this is how I watched it being made in a Chennai kitchen. Cooled dal vadas soaked in a little water first, then dipped in beaten natural yoghurt and seasoned with chilli and ground cumin are known as dahi vadas and are eaten cold. Dahi means yoghurt. Soaking vadas in water will enable them to absorb the beaten spicy yogurt better.

250g kala chana
thumb-size piece root ginger, grated
small pinch asafoetida powder (*hing*)
1 teaspoon chilli powder
100g gram flour (besan)
pinch bicarbonate of soda
3-4 tablespoons cooking oil
75g chopped onion
50g chopped coriander leaves
salt, to taste

For the dip
450g natural yoghurt, beaten
¼ teaspoon salt
1 teaspoon cumin seeds, dry roasted in a pan then ground
1 tablespoon chopped coriander leaves
1 teaspoon hot chilli sauce
1 tablespoon chopped mint leaves
2 tablespoons tamarind paste mixed with very little water

Soak the dal overnight, drain and grind in a liquidiser with the fresh ginger, asafoetida, chilli powder, and a little salt. Beat gram flour into the mixture with a pinch of bicarbonate soda to make a thick batter suitable to be dolloped gently into the pan. Heat the oil high in a large frying pan (the oil

should be about 2cm deep) and place 1 heaped teaspoon of thick batter into the oil for one vada or fritter and continue this way in batches of 5-6, turning them over and over again till golden on both sides and crisp, and until all the batter is used up adjusting the heat as you fry. You need to turn it down intermittently to achieve the colour and crispiness. After you have made all of the vadas, cool them and arrange on a plate and serve with the yoghurt dip or chutney. Mix the chopped onion and coriander leaves together in a bowl and sprinkle over the top. Vadas can be made in advance and warmed in a microwave.

To make the dip, beat the yoghurt with salt and blend it with the dry roasted cumin seeds, chopped coriander, chilli sauce, mint leaves and tamarind liquid and serve in a bowl.

Olan with Pumpkin from Kerala

Olan is Kerala's signature dish. Authenticity requires fresh coconut milk squeezed from a grated coconut. However I have used tinned coconut milk and black-eye beans here. You can soak the dried ones and boil them if you wish. Unlike other dal dishes this recipe does not use dried spices. Fresh chillies, curry leaves and good quality coconut milk add flavours to tinned beans used in this simple and quick dish.

200g pumpkin, cut into small cubes
2 green chillies, slit lengthwise
400g tin black-eye beans
400ml tin good quality coconut milk
10 fresh curry leaves
1 teaspoon coconut oil
salt, to taste

Simmer the pumpkin pieces, salt and chillies, in a pan with approximately 150ml water for five to six minutes till the pumpkin is soft. Stir in the black-eye beans and coconut milk. Mix well and leave for two more minutes then add the curry leaves and pour the coconut oil over it. Cover the pan to retain flavours and remove from the heat to serve with freshly boiled rice.

Plain or Stuffed Dosas

Dosas, which are lentil pancakes, can be a little complicated to make at home. Success depends on experience, the quality of the ingredients and the right fermentation temperature etc. Even though you can now buy the ingredients in a packet and follow the instructions to make them, freshly made dosas really are worth the effort. I have watched these dosas made in an ordinary kitchen in southern India and scribbled down the recipe and the process in my notebook. If you are going to stuff the dosa make the filling first.

300g rice
100g split and husked urid dal
¾ teaspoon ground fenugreek seeds (*methi*)
cooking oil as needed
salt, to taste

Soak the rice and the dal with the fenugreek seeds in warm water overnight. Drain off the water and grind the dal in a food processor to make a smooth batter. Leave the batter at room temperature for six to eight hours to ferment.

Warm a flat griddle pan or large frying pan and smear it with cooking oil with a basting brush. Ladle approximately three to four tablespoons batter into the centre of the pan and like making an omelette spread it around to make a circle, roughly 20cm wide. Drizzle a little more cooking oil round the edge and over it to avoid sticking to the pan. When the surface looks firm flip the pancake over. The bottom of the dosa by now should look golden. Cook the flipped dosa for another minute. It is nearly done so allow it to stay in the pan for about twenty to thirty seconds for the dosa to become crisp. Serve immediately with sambar or coconut chutney. You can also stuff plain dosas with various vegetables. The most popular filling is spiced onion and potatoes.

Spiced potato and onion filling
1 tablespoon vegetable oil
½ teaspoon nigella seeds
1 large onion, thinly sliced
3-4 medium-sized peeled potatoes

(cont...)

1 teaspoon ground turmeric
1 teaspoon ground cumin
½ teaspoon chilli powder
water, as needed
salt to taste

Heat the oil in a pan and when hot throw in the nigella seeds and toss a little to release their flavour before adding the onion. Sauté until soft. Meanwhile slice the potatoes into ½cm thick slices, and quarter each slice for quick cooking. Then add the potato slices to the pan together with the turmeric, cumin and chilli powder. Fry for a minute or so to allow the spices to blend and then add 4-6 tablespoons of water, put the lid on the saucepan, turn the heat down and allow to simmer for 8-10 minutes for the potatoes to cook. Add salt, to taste. When cooled a little, spoon the filling onto the dosa, fold or roll and serve. Always prepare fillings beforehand.

Idli

Idli (steamed rice cake) is a popular south Indian breakfast dish served with chutney and sambar. Ancient in origin, idli used to be steamed in a 20cm square piece of muslin, filled with the batter and tied at the corners and cooked in batches inside a covered pan. Now you can get a stainless steel idli steamer with ready-made mould from Asian shops for perfectly shaped circular cakes. This is a basic recipe.

300g hulled, split urid dal
100g rice
1-2 tablespoons vegetable oil
salt, to taste

Wash rice and dal separately and soak overnight.

Grind both separately then mix well vigorously and keep overnight in a warm place to ferment. Grease the idli mould with vegetable oil then pour the batter to fill ¾ of the mould then leave to steam for 20 minutes. Check it is cooked with a skewer to see if it comes out dry. Serve with sambar (page 50) and chutney of choice.

Shahjahani Dal from Hyderabad

Hyderabad, the capital of Andhra Pradesh lies at the crossroad of north and south India. As its cuisine has been influenced by the Mughals this dal dish is richly spicy and named after the emperor Shahjahan (1592-1666) who built the Taj Mahal.

300g yellow split peas
2 tablespoons ghee or clarified butter
4 cardamom pods
2 small cinnamon sticks
4-6 cloves
2 medium onions, sliced
3-4 garlic cloves, crushed
½ fresh coconut meat, sliced into 1cm pieces and
made into small cubes
½ x 400g tin coconut milk
2 tablespoons single cream
1 red and 1 green chilli, for garnishing
handful coriander leaves, chopped

Boil the split peas vigorously for five minutes in 600ml water. Skim off any froth. Turn down the heat and leave to cook till soft. Heat one and a half tablespoons ghee in a frying pan and fry the cardamom, cinnamon and cloves. As they begin to emit their aroma, add the sliced onions and fry till soft then add the garlic and toss it about briskly. Tip this mixture into the saucepan of cooked dal and simmer gently for five to six minutes. While it simmers, shallow fry the coconut cubes in the remaining ghee for two to three minutes. Drop them into the simmering dal including the ghee dregs. Now blend the coconut milk with the single cream and pour into the pan and add salt, to taste. Garnish with the whole chillies and chopped coriander leaves. Serve with pilau rice or naan bread.

Tamil Toor Dal with Okra

Okra also known as *bhindi* is a tropical vegetable with a sticky sap, which blends well with toor dal. It is a green tapering seedpod around five to six centimetres long with grooves outside and moist white round seeds inside. They are now widely available in supermarkets, both fresh and frozen. When buying okra avoid the older scaly type crops.

250g toor dal
1 teaspoon ground turmeric
1 tablespoon melted ghee
1 tablespoon coconut oil
1 teaspoon mustard seeds
2 onions, peeled and chopped finely
3 tomatoes, skinned and chopped
thumb-sized piece root ginger, peeled and grated
450g fresh tender okra pods, sliced into 2cm lengths
2 green chillies, seeded and sliced
2 red chillies, seeded and sliced
1 tablespoon tamarind paste (mixed with a cup
of warm water)
10 curry leaves
salt, to taste

Boil the dal in approximately 700ml water and skim off any scum and froth that rises to the surface. Reduce the heat, add turmeric, partially cover the pan and simmer for 25-30 minutes until the dal is soft and has broken down. Heat the ghee and the coconut oil together in a saucepan. Fry the mustard seeds briefly and before they splutter, add the chopped onions, tomatoes and grated ginger with the sliced okra. Fry them for six to eight minutes, stirring occasionally, until the okra are cooked. Add the sliced red and green chillies and a little water if necessary. Then tip the cooked dal into the saucepan of cooked okra. Pour over the tamarind liquid, season well with salt and leave to simmer for a few minutes. Crush the curry leaves a little and throw them in. Stir through and turn off the heat. Serve with boiled rice.

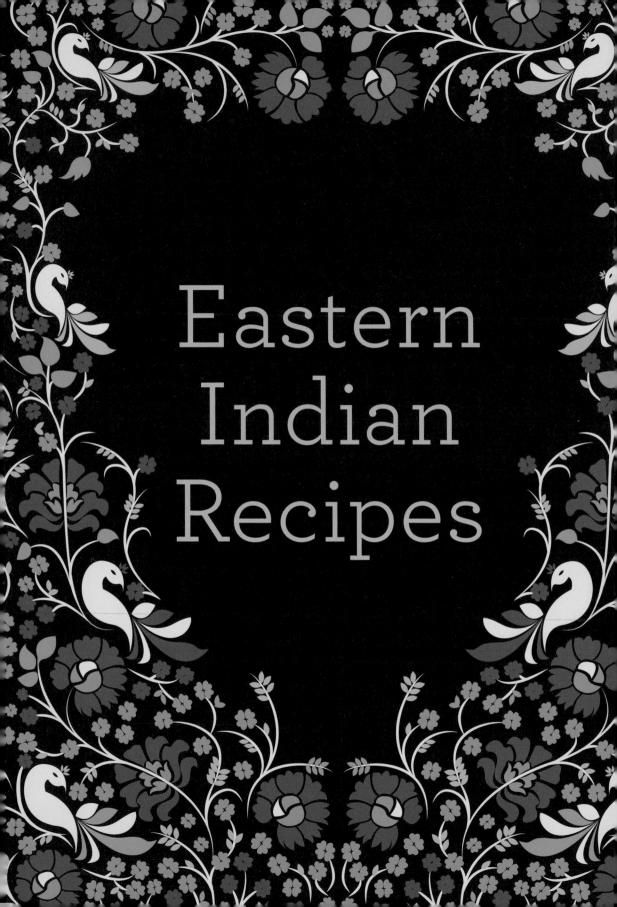

Eastern Indian Recipes

Bengali Coconut Chholar Dal

Green Mango Dal from Orissa

Elephant Apple Dal from Assam

Fish Head with Moong Dal

Moong Dal from Tripura

Bengali Masoor Dal

Moong Dal with Cauliflower

Masoor Dal with Shrimps

Whole Brown Masoor Dal with Spinach

Bengal Urid Dal

Toor Dal from Orissa

Masoor Dal with Sliced White Fish

Bengali Khichuri

Sukhno Masoor

Masoor Dal from Sylhet

Dhokar Dalna

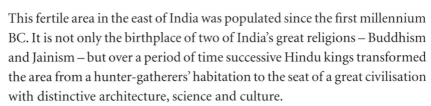

This fertile area in the east of India was populated since the first millennium BC. It is not only the birthplace of two of India's great religions – Buddhism and Jainism – but over a period of time successive Hindu kings transformed the area from a hunter-gatherers' habitation to the seat of a great civilisation with distinctive architecture, science and culture.

Nalanda – the world's first great residential university in recorded history – once stood here attracting pupils and scholars from Korea, Japan, China, Tibet, Indonesia, Persia and Turkey. Founded in the 5th century AD and destroyed in 1193 by Turkish invasion, its protected architectural site remains a historical testimony to a glorious past.

Sri Chaitayna – the founder of Vaisnavism (one of the major branches of Hinduism) and a medieval social reformer – was born here. The Vaisnavas preserve a significant vegetarian culinary legacy – particularly in the recipes of kedgeree (*khichuri*).

The eastern Indian states include West Bengal, Assam, Orissa, Manipur, Tripura and Nagaland among others. The bulk of the region lies on the east coast of India by the Bay of Bengal.

Though vegetarianism was the norm among the largely peaceful local population, the plentiful availability of fresh fish has also become a culinary favourite. However the non-Hindus and the tribal people always ate meat. Hindu religion too adapted to fish eating with qualifications and sanctions, such as not eating it on certain days of the week or during some religious rites and forbidding specific social groups.

Simplicity and moderate use of spice and fat are two significant features of cuisine from this region. Yet food cooked here is flavoursome with dal dishes augmented with fish, vegetables and fresh herbs as will be seen in the recipes I have collected.

Bengali Coconut Chholar Dal

Prior to the partition of India in 1947 Bengal was one single state. Now mostly Hindu Bengalis live in West Bengal and mainly Muslim Bengalis in Bangladesh in eastern Bengal. However this dish has been cooked for millennia in undivided Bengal and is still a favourite in both the regions.

250g yellow split Bengal gram dal (chana dal)
1 teaspoon ground cumin
1 teaspoon ground turmeric
1 teaspoon chilli powder
½ coconut, sliced and cubed like croutons
2 tablespoons cooking oil
1 tablespoon whole garam masala mix (consisting of a couple of cinnamon sticks, four cloves and four small cardamom pods)
2 bay leaves
1 teaspoon raisins
1 teaspoon ghee
salt, to taste

Boil the gram dal in approximately 700ml water with cumin, turmeric and chilli till mushy and set aside. Fry coconut cubes in the cooking oil to light brown and drain. In the same hot fat put in the whole garam masala and bay leaves. Keep frying till the aroma rises but do not burn them. In this recipe they remain whole throughout so as to release more flavour to neutralise the smell of fried coconut. Tip the cooked dal in with the spices and stir in the cubed fried coconuts and raisins. Stir in 1 teaspoon of ghee and salt, to taste. Use a hand held whisk to blend everything together and turn the heat off. The consistency should be on the thick side. Serve with luchis (page 122), rotis (page 118) or parathas (page 119).

Green Mango Dal from Orissa

Orissa has never had a culinary heritage but it is one of India's most holy pilgrimage destinations for the great temple of Jagganath. The word has been corrupted to become 'juggernaut', used to refer to the massive holy chariot pulled by devotees for an annual religious festival at the seaside city of Puri. This recipe is one of the seasonal dishes offered to the Hindu temple deity to liven his palate. The Hindus attribute divinities with human qualities of perceptions such as hunger and thirst.

250g split yellow moong dal
½ teaspoon ground turmeric
½ teaspoon chilli powder
4 small green mangoes
1 tablespoon oil
½ teaspoon nigella seeds
salt, to taste

Boil the moong dal in 600ml water in a heavy pan with turmeric and chilli powder till soft, and set aside.

Peel and slice the green mangoes lengthwise, each into eight pieces. Rub them with a pinch of salt and gently fry them in the oil until they are a little soft but not mushy. Put the black nigella seeds in the same oil and when they begin to splutter, tip the contents into the boiled dal and bring the pan back to the heat. Add a little water and salt, to taste and simmer for five minutes. This sour and watery dish is usually served as a starter with plain boiled rice and a vegetable side dish such as sag-aloo (potato and spinach curry) or aloo-gobi (potato and cauliflower curry) as a midday meal.

Elephant Apple Dal from Assam

Elephant apple is a tropical acidic fruit grown in Southeast Asia and also locally known as Chalta. The fruit is spherical with a grey-green scruffy hard rind which needs to be cracked. The sour pulp is then scooped out and cooked. This dish is popular with the people of Assam. I have also tried this recipe with two large Bramley apples grated, which gave the dish a nice British twist.

250g masoor dal
1 teaspoon ground turmeric
½ teaspoon chilli powder
Scooped out flesh from one elephant apple or use
grated cooking apples
1 tablespoon oil
½ teaspoon five spice (*panch phoran*) mix
1 teaspoon fresh root ginger, grated
salt and a little sugar to taste

Boil the dal in approximately 600ml water in a heavy pan with ground turmeric and chilli till soft, and set aside.

Collect the flesh from the fruit discarding the rind and mix it with just a pinch of turmeric and salt. Fry it in the oil gently in a pan till a little mushy. Put the five spice seeds in the same oil and when they begin to splutter, tip the contents into the boiled dal and bring the pan of dal to boil. Add a little water if needed then add sugar, grated ginger and salt to taste. Simmer for five minutes to release the flavour of ginger. Take it off the heat and use a hand whisk to blend the ingredients gently. This sweet and sour dal is usually served with plain boiled rice for the main midday lunch on a hot day.

Fish Head with Moong Dal

People in Bengal and Bangladesh prefer to cook with mustard oil extracted from tiny mustard seeds and refined. It has a strong nutty taste and a pungent aroma that complements the smell of fish. Low in saturated fat, mustard oil is now available from most Indian grocers. The stronger the scent the better is the quality. Though this authentic recipe, as served in East and West Bengal is a local favourite, it may not suit western tastes. However some of my non-Indian guests have surprised me with their liking for this dish.

500g fish head such as Rohu and Bhetki
(may be replaced with grey mullet, carp or sea bass)
½ teaspoon salt
½ teaspoon ground turmeric
1 tablespoon good mustard oil
200g green or yellow split moong dal
1 teaspoon ground turmeric
½ teaspoon chilli powder
½ teaspoon cumin seeds
2 bay leaves
pinch of asafoetida (*hing*)
4 cardamom pods, lightly crushed
2 onions, chopped
2 deseeded green chillies, for flavouring and garnishing

Clean the fish head and cut into four pieces. Rub a little salt and the half teaspoon of turmeric all over them. Set them aside for a while before frying the pieces briefly in mustard oil.

Dry fry or toast the dal in the saucepan without oil till the nutty flavour emerges then boil in about 600ml of warm water with ground turmeric and chilli powder till soft, and set aside.

Fry the cumin seeds, bay leaves, asafoetida and cardamom in a little oil in another saucepan. As they begin to splutter, add the chopped onions and slowly brown them.

Now pour the cooked dal into this pan and gently add the fish heads. Blend well with a whisk to help them disintegrate and simmer for five more minutes. Dunk in a couple of deseeded green chillies slit lengthwise to

release fresh flavour. Serve with rice. It is worth noting perhaps that local people always use their fingers to eat this dish so that they can pick out the fish bones while eating.

Moong Dal from Tripura

Tripura is India's third smallest state in the northeast of the country bordering Bangladesh and has a rich tradition of music, dance and handicrafts. Its cuisine is akin to both Assam and Bengal – fresh, simple and delicate. This frugal dish is often served in the temples to the devotees of *Tripureswari* – the presiding deity of Tripura. It is wholesome, tasty, and cooked throughout eastern India.

250g moong dal
1 teaspoon freshly crushed turmeric roots if available,
(or make a paste with 2 teaspoons ground turmeric with 1 tablespoon
of warm water, to be stirred in with the tomatoes)
2 tomatoes, cut into small pieces
1 tablespoon cooking oil
1 teaspoon five spice mix (*panch phoran*) or cumin seeds as alternative
1 teaspoon fresh root ginger, crushed to a paste
2 dried whole chillies
salt, to taste

Boil the moong dal with turmeric root if using, if not add turmeric paste later (see below) in 700ml of water. As it starts to boil, turn the heat down and simmer for 20 minutes with the lid slightly ajar and skim off any rising scum. When the dal looks mushy stir in the tomatoes with the turmeric paste and take it off the heat. Set aside.

Pour the oil into a separate saucepan. When the oil is hot first add the five-spice mixture (alternatively you can use cumin seeds instead of the five spices for a different flavour) and then the ginger paste and fry gently. When the aroma from the fried spices rises, tip the cooked dal into the pan and throw in the whole dried chillies. Stir thoroughly with a whisk and add salt, to taste. Serve with boiled rice.

Bengali Masoor Dal

The ubiquitous red lentil – husked and split – is known as masoor dal in India. This is the first dal I cooked in England and since then it has become a staple in my kitchen. My mother often cooked it the following way and now my daughter too has learnt to prepare this dal as well as her Nan. This simple recipe is a distinct culinary link to my family wherever they may be and it is a real crowd pleaser with guests too.

250g masoor dal
1 teaspoon ground turmeric
1 teaspoon chilli powder
1 teaspoon ground cumin
2 large onions
3-4 garlic cloves
1 tablespoon cooking oil or ghee
1 tablespoon tomato puree
25g finely chopped spring onions or red onions, for garnishing

Bring the masoor dal to boil in 750ml of water in a saucepan with the turmeric, chilli and cumin. Turn the heat low and simmer gently for 20 minutes with the lid slightly ajar to avoid froth bubbling over. Add a little more water if needed while simmering. Stir the dal from time to time to prevent it sticking to the bottom of the pan. Take this off the heat when the consistency looks almost like mushy peas.

Slice and chop the onions and finely grate or crush the cloves of garlic. Heat the cooking oil or ghee in a frying pan. Gently fry the onions on a low heat until soft, add the garlic and stir it into a paste till aromatic but not burnt.

Pour the fried onions and garlic into the pan of dal and bring it to simmer for a couple more minutes. Stir in the tomato puree, salt and pepper.

Simmer for two more minutes. Serve at the table in a tureen or in individual bowls garnished with finely chopped spring onions or red onions. Eat with rice or bread or have it, thinned down if necessary with more water, simply as dal soup.

Moong Dal with Cauliflower

Originating in the Middle East cauliflower migrated to India and took to the soil mainly as a seasonal vegetable. This is a favourite winter dish. The cooks serve the thicker version of this recipe with puris and thinner one with boiled rice for a midday meal. A spicier richer version of this dish with five mixes of dals is cooked in the north.

250g small, split yellow moong dal
1 teaspoon ground turmeric
1 teaspoon ground cumin
1 teaspoon chilli powder (optional)
1 medium cauliflower, divided into small florets
2 tablespoons ghee
4 small green cardamom pods
2 small cinnamon sticks
1 tablespoon fresh root ginger, grated
2 tablespoons tomato puree
1 tablespoon fresh chopped coriander leaves
salt, to taste

Dry fry or toast the dal in a deep frying pan without oil till the nutty aroma rises and set aside for a couple of minutes. Pour 700ml of warm water into a heavy saucepan, add the toasted dal and bring to a boil. Turn the heat down, add the ground turmeric, cumin and chilli to it, put the lid on and let it simmer for 20 minutes. Keep watching so it does not become dry and add water if necessary. Add the cauliflower florets when the dal is soft and cook for four more minutes. Set aside.

Put the ghee into a deep frying pan. When hot, crush the cardamom pods, split the cinnamon sticks and toss them in. Then add the crushed ginger with tomato puree and blend with a whisk. As the aroma rises tip them into the pan of cooked dal and stir well. Turn the heat off. Sprinkle with the coriander leaves on top and immediately put the lid on to retain the flavour. Serve with rice or unleavened bread, such as parathas (page 119) or roti (page 118).

Masoor Dal with Shrimps

Shrimps are abundant in the fresh and salty rivers and lakes in eastern India and are usually caught when 2-3cm long. Asia supplies 75 per cent of larger shrimps consumed in the west as prawns. Often children in small villages can be seen catching shrimps with small impromptu nets made from rags. They are a cheap source of protein for the poor. This is a very tasty and popular dish.

250g masoor dal
225g shelled (locals prefer unshelled) shrimps
2 tablespoons ghee
2 large onions, chopped
1 teaspoon ground turmeric
1 teaspoon chilli powder
1 teaspoon ground cumin
1 tablespoon fresh root ginger, grated
4 garlic cloves, pulverised
1 tablespoon fresh chopped spring onions
salt, to taste

Bring the masoor dal to boil in 700ml of water in a saucepan. Turn the heat low and simmer gently for 20 minutes with the lid slightly ajar to avoid froth bubbling over. When cooked, set aside.

Rub in a pinch of turmeric and a pinch of salt to the shrimps and leave on the side.

In another saucepan melt the ghee and fry the onions in it. When the onions are soft, stir in turmeric, chilli and cumin and fry gently. As the oil begins to separate add the crushed ginger and garlic and wait till the masala mixture releases its aroma. Now tip the cooked dal into it and blend with a hand whisk. Bring it up to a boil. Add the prepared shrimps. Cover the pan and simmer for two to three minutes till the shrimps are cooked. Turn off the heat. Sprinkle the chopped spring onions on top, cover and take off the heat. This is usually served with boiled rice.

Whole Brown Masoor Dal with Spinach

Arab traders brought spinach to the Malabar coasts in south India and from there it rapidly took root and spread all over the country. The tropical climate and fertile soil of the land facilitated the cultivation and soon it became an indispensible part of cooking culture. Two varieties of spinach are available in India – one has a red stem and the other is entirely green. I often cook this easy, recipe at home as it's so nourishing and easy to prepare – perfect after a long and tiring day.

250g whole brown masoor dal (with husk)
1 teaspoon ground turmeric
1 teaspoon chilli powder
1 tablespoon tomato puree
1 tablespoon cooking oil
2 large onions, chopped
3-4 garlic cloves, crushed
100g whole leaf spinach (fresh or frozen)

Bring the whole brown masoor dal to boil in approximately 700ml of water in a saucepan. Turn the heat low and simmer gently for 20 minutes with the lid slightly ajar to avoid froth bubbling over. When cooked, stir in the turmeric, chilli and tomato puree and let it simmer for five more minutes. Set aside.

Take a frying pan and heat the oil. Fry the onions till soft and add the crushed garlic till aromatic. Tip the onion and garlic into the pan of boiled dal and bring it to the boil again. When it begins to bubble, put the washed spinach in and simmer for two more minutes and turn the heat off. This wholesome dish can be served as a soup with strips of warm naan bread.

Bengal Urid Dal

Originating in Asia, urad or urid dal is de-husked and split. When cooked it can become gooey. Bengalis prefer urid dal until it achieves a texture similar to that of macaroni cheese. They do not always dry fry the dals but boil straight to retain viscosity. To avoid this, you can dry fry the dal in a pan till the grains are lightly brown and give out a lovely nutty smell. Many Bengalis and Bangladeshis relish this nostalgic gluey dish with a squeeze of fresh lime, mashed potato mixed with finely sliced raw onion, whole green chilli to bite and boiled rice. However this dal might be an acquired taste for westerners!

200g split urid dal
1 teaspoon ground turmeric
1 teaspoon chilli powder
1 tablespoon cooking oil
1 tablespoon fresh root ginger, grated
1 tablespoon ground fennel seed
pinch asafoetida powder (*hing*, optional)
1 whole dried chilli
½ bunch spring onions, sliced
slice of lime
salt, to taste

Bring the split urid dal up to the boil in approximately 800ml of water in a saucepan with the turmeric and chilli. Turn the heat low and simmer gently for 40 minutes with the lid slightly ajar to avoid froth bubbling over. Add more water if required. When soft set aside.

Heat the oil in another saucepan and when hot put the grated ginger, ground fennel seeds and a pinch of asafoetida into the oil and fry till aromatic. Put in one whole dried chilli just before tipping the cooked urid into the pan. Be aware if you leave the chilli longer in hot oil, it will split and splutter. So don't! You only need the flavour of the chilli and not the heat.

Now tip the dal into the saucepan and blend with a hand whisk and cook for five more minutes. Serve with sliced spring onions and a slice of lime on a plate of basmati rice.

Toor Dal from Orissa

This ancient crop, also known as pigeon pea, grows abundantly in the tropical deciduous forests of Orissa. Toor has been an important source of protein for the impoverished local vegetarian population for centuries. It is drought resistant and suitable for multiple cropping.

250g toor dal (round, hulled, split, oily or dry)
1 teaspoon ground turmeric
1 teaspoon chilli powder
1 tablespoon cooking oil
1 tablespoon grated fresh root ginger
pinch asafoetida powder (*hing*, optional)
2 tomatoes, skinned and pulped
1 tablespoon chopped onion
1 tablespoon chopped coriander leaves
salt, to taste

Boil the toor dal in approximately 800ml of water with the turmeric and chilli and set aside.

In a frying pan heat the oil. When hot put in the grated ginger and asafoetida and cook till aromatic. Add the tomatoes and fry till the oil is released. Tip the mixture into the pan of cooked dal and bring it up to a boil. Blend it with a hand whisk and simmer for five more minutes. Consistency should be on the thick side like baked beans. Take it off the heat. Garnish the dish with chopped onions and coriander leaves and cover to retain flavour. Serve with naan or chapatti (page 118) or parathas (page 119).

Masoor Dal with Sliced White Fish

I was curious to find this dish on the menu of a seaside hotel in Puri in Orissa because usually in the east of India, dal is served with deep fried fish. The cook told me that this dish has evolved as a healthier option to the deep fried fish and has become a popular choice with tourists since the 1990s.

200g split pink masoor dal (red lentils)
1 teaspoon chilli powder
1 teaspoon ground turmeric
1 teaspoon ground cumin
400g fish fillets, sliced into 2-3cm pieces (cod, haddock or pollock may be used instead of the Indian Rohu or Bhetki)
2 tablespoons ghee or clarified butter
2 large onions, chopped
1 tablespoon freshly grated root ginger
2 bay leaves
2 green chillies, deseeded and sliced
salt, to taste

Bring the masoor dal to boil in a saucepan in 700ml of water. Turn the heat low and simmer gently for 20 minutes with the lid slightly ajar to avoid froth bubbling over. When cooked add the chilli powder, turmeric and cumin and cook for five more minutes, then set aside.

Smear the fish fillets with a little turmeric and a pinch of salt and shallow fry in a pan or steam them and set aside.

In another saucepan heat the ghee and when hot, add the chopped onions. As they begin to brown add the grated ginger and the bay leaves. When the aroma rises, pour in the cooked dal and the sliced chillies and simmer for five more minutes. Before taking it off the heat gently put in the cooked fish. Turn the heat off. Let it stand for a couple of minutes before serving with boiled rice.

Bengali Khichuri

Popularly known as kedgeree, this humble rice-lentil dish was often prepared outdoors by the Indian cooks for their itinerant British Civil Service masters working away in a remote place. It became a renowned Anglo-Indian breakfast dish in Victorian England – with the addition of fish. This authentic recipe is a staple for heavy monsoon days in Bengal when the usual outdoor market stalls disappear.

100g moong or masoor dal
100g white or brown rice
1 tablespoon cooking oil
1 large onion, sliced and chopped
1 tablespoon freshly grated ginger
1 teaspoon ground garam masala
1½ teaspoons ground turmeric
2 tomatoes, chopped
2 bay leaves
1 teaspoon ghee or clarified butter
2 green chillies, sliced diagonally
300g cauliflower florets (optional)
150g fresh or frozen peas (optional)
2 large potatoes cut in 2cm cubes (optional)

Wash the dal and rice separately and leave them to dry on two flat plates.

In a saucepan fry the onion in the oil till soft and then add the grated ginger and garam masala and fry together. As the aroma rises add the rice and lentils with turmeric into the spice mixture and fry for another couple of minutes for them to blend well. Parboil a full kettle on the side and pour the warm water into the pot. The level of water should be about 3-4cm above the dal-rice mixture. Bring this up to the boil and leave to simmer on a low heat until the grains are cooked. It should take about 15-20 minutes. Now add the chopped tomatoes. Like cooking risotto you need to check constantly that it is not sticking and add more water if needed. Throw in a couple of bay leaves and the ghee and blend well. Leave for another couple of minutes. Add the slit green chillies.

Some people add small cauliflower florets, fresh peas and small cubed potatoes at this point but that is optional. When everything is cooked properly take it off the heat and serve with poppadums (page 116) and lime or ginger pickle (page 126).

Sukhno Masoor

The word *sukhno* or *sukha* means dry and hence the name of this recipe is dry mashed masoor dal. A favourite with everyone from Indian pavement dwellers to homesick students; this is the ultimate austerity recipe. For authenticity one needs to use mustard oil but butter works just as well for me.

250g whole masoor dal
1 teaspoon ground turmeric
3-4 garlic cloves, crushed
1 tablespoon mustard oil or a teaspoon of good butter
2 large onions, chopped
2 fresh green chillies, sliced and deseeded if preferred
½ teaspoon freshly ground peppercorns

Bring the dal to boil in approximately 600ml water with turmeric and crushed garlic cloves and simmer on a low heat until it looks like mashed potato. Throughout the course of cooking keep stirring. Do not let it stick to the bottom of the pan. Take it off the heat and leave it to cool a little. When moderately warm, stir the mustard oil (or butter), chopped onions and sliced chillies into the dry mush. Add salt, to taste. Serve it with a little boiled rice and a bowl of cucumber raita (page 126). If you do not want to make a raita, have it with pickled lime and mix the rice with one teaspoon of quality butter and the freshly ground peppercorns. It tastes delicious.

Masoor Dal from Sylhet

Sylhet is a major city in Bangladesh and played an important role in the Bangladesh Liberation war during the 1970s. Migration from Sylhet to Britain began in the days of the East India Company, who employed Sylhetis as lascars (sailors). I tasted this dal recently at a Bangladeshi friend's home in London who informed me that this frugal but delicious dal is a staple in Sylhet.

250g split masoor dal (red lentils)
1 teaspoon ground turmeric
1 teaspoon chilli powder
1 tablespoon tomato puree
2 fresh whole green chillies
1 teaspoon cooking oil
3-4 garlic cloves, sliced
2 large onions, sliced
salt, to taste

Bring the masoor dal to boil in 650ml of water in a saucepan with the turmeric and chilli. Turn the heat low and simmer gently for 20 minutes with the lid slightly ajar to avoid froth bubbling over. Add a little more water if needed while simmering. Stir the dal from time to time to prevent it sticking to the bottom of the pan. Stir in the tomato puree, the fresh whole green chillies and salt. Take the pan off the heat when the consistency looks similar to that of mushy peas.

Heat a teaspoonful of cooking oil in a frying pan. When very hot, fry the garlic slices briskly for 10 seconds to release the aroma and toss them over the cooked dal. Put the same oily frying pan back on the hob and fry the onions with no extra oil. The technique is to brown them in their own moisture. So you need to control the heat from high to low with constant stirring to avoid burning. You can sprinkle on a few drops of water to keep it moist. They will take time to brown – approximately 10-15 minutes. Serve the dal in a tureen or in individual bowls with the freshly browned onions floated on top. Tastes great with boiled rice or simply as dal soup.

Dhokar Dalna

This is Bengal's vegetarian signature dish. The Bengali word 'Dhoka' means fake because this spicy potato-lentil cake curry looks as if it contains meat or fish pieces rather than just humble lentils! 'Dalna' is a variety of curry. Be warned this dish is a bit fiddly and tricky to prepare. You need patience, knack and time. You may not succeed at first, but it's worth persevering for a delicious result in time.

For the Dhokar pieces
250g split peas or chana dal
thumb-sized piece of ginger, grated
100g grated coconut, fresh or creamed
pinch of sugar
2 tablespoons gram flour (besan)
salt, to taste
4-6 tablespoons cooking oil

For the Dalna curry
250g baby potatoes cut into halves
1 teaspoon cumin seeds
2 bay leaves
½ teaspoon ground turmeric
1 teaspoon chilli powder
2 teaspoons ground cumin
2 teaspoons tomato puree
1 teaspoon ready-made ground garam masala
1 teaspoon ghee
salt, to taste

Soak the dal overnight, strain and grind the mixture with grated ginger, coconut, sugar, besan to bind, and salt. In a warm wok brushed with a little oil toss the mixture in and put it on a low heat stirring constantly. Add a little more oil if needed. The object is to turn the mixture into a cooked dough that does not stick to the wok. Be patient, watchful and work at it for about 10 to 15 minutes. Take it off the heat and when cooled, spread the dough over a dinner plate smeared in oil, making it roughly 2cm thick. Cut the dough into 2-3cm diamond or square shapes with a knife. Lift them out gently with a flat blade knife and shallow fry just to crisp them, 2 to 3 at a time in a pan with cooking oil until the dough is finished. You need to control the heat and be very careful not to break them while frying. Place them on kitchen towel to drain off any excess oil and set aside ready to put into your dalna or serve on their own as savoury snacks. The dhoka pieces can be reheated in a microwave.

To make the dalna, fry the potatoes in the left over oil in the same pan to brown them a little, then throw in the cumin seeds and bay leaves. As they begin to sizzle add turmeric, chilli, cumin and blend well with the potatoes. Add tomato puree. As the aroma rises, add enough warm water to cover the potatoes and leave to cook. When potatoes are cooked add the garam masala, ghee and salt to taste, and leave to simmer for another minute, then gently put the dhokas in making sure that they do not break as you drop them in. Cook for two more minutes. Alternatively you can lay the dhokas in a tureen, ladle the potato curry over them and microwave for a minute. Remember the dhokas absorb liquid so the gravy will reduce in time if left too long before serving. Serve with boiled rice.

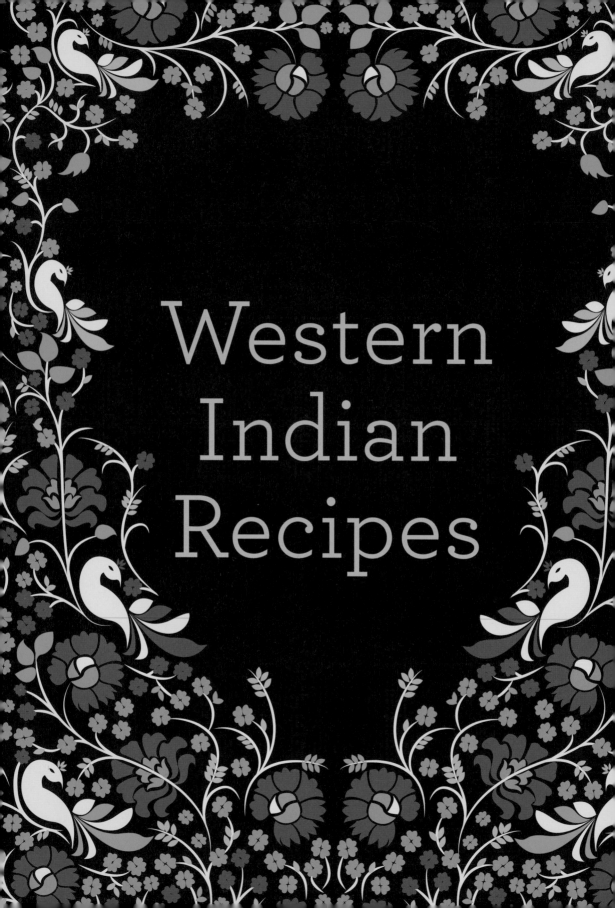

Western Indian Recipes

Everyday Goan Dal

Everyday Dal from Gujarat

Warm Sprouting Moong Bean Dal

Gujarati Kadhi

Dhansak

Split Pea Dal Puri

Dal Dumplings with Potatoes

Goan Prawn and Coconut Dal

Dal with Five Kinds of Vegetable

Dal Bukhara

Moong Dal Laddu

Spinach with Toor Dal

Though most of western India is now very urban and highly industrialised, it has a rich traditional history. Stretching from the deserts bordering Pakistan to the tropical slopes of Maharashtra, it is also the home to some of the country's most important historical sites like Mahabalipuram (Mallapuram) – with ancient open-air sculptures – and Tanjore (Thanjavur) with a World Heritage temple.

Western Indian states include Maharashtra, Gujarat, Goa, parts of Rajasthan and the union territories of Daman and Diu. The general climate varies between wet, tropical wet and dry, and semi arid, though the coastal regions experience little seasonal variations.

The dry climate in parts of western India means fewer vegetables are grown in this part of the country and, as is often the case, creative cooks have shown that necessity is indeed the mother of invention. For example, to compensate for the lack of fresh vegetables all year round, western Indians have become expert at preparing pickles and chutneys to add variety to their meals. Despite its difficult climate, this region probably has the most diverse styles of food in all India. For example, Goa is generally known for its Portuguese influenced Vindaloo dish, but its lush green coastline also provides large quantities of fresh fish and seafood for the locals. Rajasthani food is spicy and largely vegetarian but includes many

delicious meat dishes like the hot and spicy red meat curry, while Gujarat's traditionally vegetarian cuisine is also known for its 'pinch of jaggery'(a kind of unrefined cane sugar) added to most dishes! Some Gujarati dishes can be chilli hot too.

Cosmopolitan Maharashtra on the other hand is partly coastal and lush, partly inland and arid so the culinary taste varies accordingly. Peanuts and coconut are important ingredients for dishes from this area.

Gujarat and Rajasthan harvest corn, various dal lentils and gram – a variety of chickpea, chillies, nuts and sugar cane. Chief dairy products are butter, ghee, buttermilk, yoghurt and paneer cheese.

Favourite spices and ingredients used in western India's cooking are sun-dried red chillies, cane sugar, palm jaggery, sesame seeds, coconut, peanuts, vinegar, fish and pork. Gujarati culture includes both Hindu and Islamic influence. The Parsis who migrated to Gujarat from Iran about 1000 years ago have also influenced the cuisine. *Thali* (a large plate) is a Gujarati style of meal consisting of as many as ten different bowls of vegetables including dal or sambar with rice, dosas or parathas and a dessert dish.

The dishes collected here reflect the culinary diversity of this region.

Everyday Goan Dal

This recipe is yet another example of India's simple and diverse dal cuisine. It uses *hing*. *Hing* is Indian asafoetida. Raw asafoetida from Kabul in Afghanistan is considered the best. It smells like rotten strong cheese but don't let that put you off – when added to hot oil, it adds depth and flavour to a dish and is known for its digestive and anti-flatulence properties (useful if you are relatively new to dal!). The Indian asafoetida can be found in Asian shops and you need to ask for *hing*.

200g toor dal
½ teaspoon ground turmeric
2 tablespoons ghee
1 teaspoon mustard seeds
1 teaspoon asafoetida (*hing*, if available)
thumb-sized piece fresh root ginger, finely grated
2 dried red chillies, roughly crushed
1 teaspoon cumin seeds
2 large tomatoes, peeled and pulped
45g fresh, chopped coriander leaves
salt, to taste

Boil the dal in approximately 500ml water with the turmeric and set aside.

Pour the ghee into a pan and place on the heat, when warmed add the mustard seeds. As they begin to splutter add the *hing* first followed by the grated ginger and crushed red chillies and fry for about 10 seconds. Gently pour the cooked dal over it and cook for 5 minutes more. Add the pulped tomatoes and cook for one more minute before turning off the heat. Garnish with chopped coriander. Serve with warm rice.

Everyday Dal from Gujarat

Gujarat is home to more vegetarians than anywhere in India. Guajarati people also make varieties of wonderful pickles and crunchy spicy savoury nibbles like *chevda/chivda/chewda* – a dry mixture consisting mainly of puffed rice, rice flakes, peanuts, sultanas, fried lentils, fried coconut flakes and roasted dal flour noodles seasoned with various spices. It is packaged and sold here as Bombay Mix. *Gathia* – deep fried Gujarati breakfast bread made from spiced gram flour dough – can also form part of *chevda* mix when broken into bits. Modern Gujarat is mainly Hindu. It is a prosperous state strong with agricultural and industrial sectors and also a major culinary region of India.

200g toor dal or split moong dal
1 teaspoon ground turmeric
1 teaspoon chilli powder
100g sweet potato, peeled and cubed
2 tablespoons ground peanuts
1 tablespoon ghee
1 tablespoon cooking oil
½ teaspoon mustard seed
½ teaspoon cumin seed
thumb-sized piece root ginger, grated
pinch asafoetida (*hing*)
10-12 fenugreek leaves (*methi*) (available in some large supermarkets)
1 tablespoon chopped tomato
50g palm jaggery
1 tablespoon lemon juice
salt, to taste

Boil the dal in 700ml water with the turmeric and chilli powder in a saucepan and set aside. In a *karahi* or wok, cook the cubed sweet potatoes with peanuts with a sprinkle of water but no oil. When cooked, mash it up and blend it with the cooked dal.

Heat the ghee and oil in another saucepan and fry the mustard and cumin seeds together. As they begin to splutter add the grated ginger, asafoetida and dried fenugreek leaves. When aromatic, tip the cooked dal and potato into the mixture with the spices. Add a little water and cook for a couple of minutes. Now stir in the chopped tomato, jaggery, lemon juice and salt, to taste. Blend them well, and cook for a minute more. Serve with boiled rice.

Warm Sprouting Moong Bean Dal

Moong (mung) bean sprouts have been grown in India for thousands of years and are prized for their nutritional value. I have been a little wary of cooking sprouted bean dishes in the past but now their availability in many supermarkets has prompted me to include this fresh and crunchy dish from a Marathi kitchen.

150g whole green moong beans or 300g bean sprouts
1 tablespoon cooking oil
¼ teaspoon mustard seeds
200g grated fresh coconut or grated block of creamed coconut
2 garlic cloves, pulverized
pinch of asafoetida (*hing*)
4-5 curry leaves
2 green chillies, diagonally split
45g chopped coriander leaves
1 tablespoon juice of lime
salt, to taste

Soak the whole mung beans in plenty of fresh water overnight. In the morning drain the water and cover loosely with a muslin. Leave enough room for them to grow and place them in a warm place till they sprout. They should do so the next day. Alternatively buy fresh sprouted beans (bean sprouts) from ethnic supermarkets.

Heat the oil in a pan and fry the mustard seeds, grated coconut, crushed garlic and asafoetida till aromatic. Now add the freshly sprouted beans and stir-fry so that they still remain a crisp. Sprinkle in a little water while frying to avoid sticking if necessary. Now put the curry leaves and the slit green chillies in. Take it off the heat and mix in the chopped coriander leaves and the lime juice and cover to preserve the flavour. Serve soon as a starter or side dish with kadhi (page 100) or vadas (page 59) and boiled rice.

Gujarati Kadhi

Kadhi is a liquid sour yoghurt/buttermilk preparation made with gram flour to stimulate palates. This simple and easy recipe is a testimony to the success of Gujarati cuisine to bring together contrasting tastes. Incidentally, some cookery writers think Kadhi is the origin of the Anglicized version of the word curry.

400ml natural yoghurt
60g gram flour (besan)
¼ teaspoon ground turmeric
¼ teaspoon ground cumin
thumb-sized piece root ginger
2 fresh green chillies, finely sliced
handful fresh coriander leaves, chopped
2 tablespoons cooking oil
salt, to taste

For seasoning
¼ teaspoon cumin seeds
¼ teaspoon mustard seeds
4-6 curry leaves
pinch of asafoetida (*hing*)

In a saucepan beat the yoghurt with 500ml of water, add the gram flour, salt, turmeric and cumin and blend well.

Pulverize the root ginger, green chillies and coriander leaves and mix together.

On a low heat gently bring the yoghurt and the gram flour mixture to a simmer for 2 minutes stirring constantly. Now add the ginger-chilli-coriander paste to it. Boil the mixture for 5 minutes, stirring constantly, and set aside.

Heat the oil in a pan and fry the seasoning spices. As they begin to splutter, pour the warm seasoning mix over the cooked kadhi and serve with warm boiled rice.

Dhansak

This rich slow-cooked Persian inspired meat dish uses four kinds of lentils with tender goat meat or lamb. Traditionally it was cooked in clay ovens. Meat combined with dals, vegetables and a taste of sugariness is a Parsee speciality. The word *dhan* means wealth in Sanskrit hence it is a dish for the wealthy. 'Dhan' should not be confused with its homonym meaning 'rice grain'. The two kinds of tadkas used in this recipe help to maintain the flavours throughout cooking.

25g split gram dal
25g split moong dal
25g split masoor dal
25g split oily toor dal
4 tablespoons ghee
400g lean lamb, cubed
2 large onions, finely chopped
3 garlic cloves, pulverised
2 fresh tomatoes, skinned and pulped
2 green chillies, sliced
thumb-sized piece root ginger, grated
100g aubergine, cubed
100g pumpkin, cubed
100g fresh spinach, coarsely chopped
1 tablespoon jaggery or brown sugar
Juice 1 lime
45g freshly chopped coriander leaves

Tadka 1
(whole grain spices <u>with no water</u>)
1 teaspoon cumin seeds
seeds from one large brown cardamom pod
(available in Asian grocers)
4-5cm piece cinnamon bark, split
½ teaspoon black mustard seeds

Tadka 2
(ground spices and mixed with water)
1 teaspoon turmeric
1 teaspoon ground cumin
½ teaspoon ground fenugreek seeds
½ teaspoon chilli powder

Preheat the oven to 200°C/400°F/gas 6.

Boil the dals together in 600ml water till mushy and set aside. Heat half the ghee in a pan and fry the meat for 5-6 minutes to seal the flavour and set aside. Heat the rest of the ghee in another pan and stir fry the Tadka 1 briefly and set aside. Now mix the Tadka 2 with a little water to make a paste and add it to the pan with Tadka 1, put it on the heat and add the onions and garlic and fry altogether. Now add all the fried contents to the seared meat and mix well. Transfer it into a large casserole and put the lid on. Put the casserole in the hot oven for 30 minutes. Check two to three times to see if it's drying out and add water if necessary. When the meat is tender add the pulped tomatoes, mushed dal, green chillies, grated ginger, all the vegetables (aubergine, pumpkin, spinach) and mix well. Give it 20 minutes more in the oven then add the jaggery, lime juice, chopped coriander leaves and salt, to taste. Turn the oven off and leave it there for 15 minutes. Now the dish is ready to serve with pilau rice (page 120) or parathas (page 119).

Split Pea Dal Puri

Dal Puri – an unleavened flat bread stuffed with seasoned lentils – is a complex preparation but worth the effort. This recipe involves grinding the dals to make flour for the filling. Dal Puri is often made at home as a special treat but is also widely available in Indian restaurants. Variations of this recipe migrated to other parts of the world with the Guajarati population. It is also known as stuffed parathas, or stuffed puri or kochuri. Dal Puri can also be made with a spiced gram flour (besan) filling to skip soaking and grinding the dal but it tastes better with freshly ground dal.

For the dough
450g chapatti flour or *atta* (durum wheat flour)
½ teaspoon cooking oil
pinch of salt

For the filling
200g split peas
1 teaspoon ground cumin
½ teaspoon chilli powder
1 teaspoon cumin seeds
½ teaspoon cooking oil

For frying
1-2 tablespoons cooking oil
4-5 tablespoons melted ghee

salt, to taste

Soak the split peas overnight, drain off any excess liquid and grind into a smooth paste. Set aside.

Place the *atta* in a bowl (saving a little flour to dust the rolling board later) with half a teaspoon of cooking oil and a pinch of salt. Gradually add water a few drops at a time and knead the mixture until it becomes a soft and malleable dough. Take your time kneading (15-20 minutes) as the longer you knead the softer the dal puris will be. Once the dough is prepared, set aside at room temperature for 20 minutes.

Now mix the melted ghee and cooking oil together for frying. Put one tablespoon of ghee-oil mixture in a *karahi* or wok and pour in the ground split pea paste with the cumin, chilli powder and a little salt and stir-fry gently to avoid the mixture sticking to the pan. You can add a little water if needed and stir constantly. It should not take more than 4-5 minutes to cook. Set aside to cool. Now dry fry the cumin seeds in a pan and when cool grind them and mix well with the dry cooked dal paste. This will enhance its flavour.

Save a thumb-sized piece of dough for sealing any leaks, and then divide the dough into 8 small balls. Divide the cooked dal paste into 8 smaller balls. Take one dough ball and make a rough cup shape with both palms and fingers like a potter. Place one cooked smaller dal ball at the centre of it then close it up with fingertips and seal with a little water. Repeat this till all the dough balls are done.

Next, dust one dough ball with a little flour and roll it out on a board into a 8-10cm wide circle making sure that the dal paste does not leak out. This is a bit fiddly but if it does, carefully seal the leak with a bit of dough before frying.

Mix the cooking oil and the melted ghee together and smear a large frying pan with the ghee-oil mixture and heat well. When hot, place one rolled out dal puri on the pan and spoon over approximately ¼ teaspoon of frying fat and pat with a wooden spatula to cook for 30 seconds to 1 minute, then turn over to cook the other side to ensure that it is cooked through. The dal puri should be golden brown on each side with some brown spots and you will get the fried smell. When cooked set aside on a plate and cover with foil to retain heat. Make the rest the same way and serve fresh or microwaved later with a tamarind chutney (page 128) or lime pickle.

Dal Dumplings with Potatoes

Since I ate this spicy, tasty dish some years ago at a get-together in the home of a Gujarati friend, originally from Sindh (now in Pakistan), I often make it at home. The technique is to get the right mixture for the dough so that it does not break while shallow frying. I use gram flour to bind the dumplings and often steam, cool and then shallow fry.

200g gram dal
200g toor dal
6-8 small potatoes
2 green chillies, chopped
1 tablespoon fine gram flour (besan)
1 large onion, finely chopped
½ teaspoon cumin seeds
1½ teaspoons ground cumin
thumb-sized piece root ginger, grated
2 large tomatoes, peeled and chopped
2 tablespoons chopped fresh coriander
cooking oil
salt, to taste

Soak the dals in warm water for a couple of hours. Boil the potatoes, peel and leave to cool. Grind the dals into a thick and coarse paste with the chopped chillies. Add the gram flour and the chopped onion to the paste and make walnut-sized balls or patties with the palms of your hands smeared in oil. Flatten them a little like burgers. Make sure they are bonded well so they do not split when you fry them. Gram flour should help to bind. Gently shallow fry them. Set aside on a dish lined with a sheet of kitchen roll.

Pour a tablespoon of oil into a pan and throw in the cumin seeds. As they agitate put in the boiled potatoes. Stir them in with the ground cumin, grated ginger and the pulverized tomatoes. As the smell of fried spices rises, add 2-3 cups of water – just enough to cover the potatoes – and leave to simmer for a minute with the lid on. Gently drop in the dal dumplings one by one and simmer for 5 more minutes. Add a bit more water, as the dumplings will have absorbed some liquid and salt, to taste. Turn off the heat, sprinkle with chopped coriander and keep covered. Serve with rice or rotis (page 118).

Goan Prawn and Coconut Dal

Goa's estuarine eco-system is suitable for the habitation of fresh water prawns. Small shrimps there can often reach about 8-10cm in length to be regarded as prawns.

The locals use fresh ingredients for this classic dish. But in London I have used tinned coconut milk with a dash of fresh ginger and it worked very well.

Coconut oil extracted from its inner flesh is very heat-stable, suitable for cooking at high temperatures like frying. It is also slow to oxidize and resistant to rancidity. However it does contain high levels of saturated fat so it's worth mixing with the vegetable oil to reduce some of the fat content. People in India now use sesame oil (also known as gingili) oil instead.

50g split moong dal
50g toor dal
2 tablespoons coconut oil or sesame oil
2 large onions, finely chopped
400g peeled prawns
½ teaspoon ground turmeric
thumb-sized piece root ginger, finely grated
2 fresh green chillies, sliced
200ml tinned coconut milk
45g fresh, chopped coriander leaves
salt, to taste

Boil the dals in approximately 200-300ml water and set aside. Pour the oil in a pan and stir fry the onions a little. Dust the prawns with the ground turmeric and add them to the pan and toss them rapidly for about 20 seconds, stir in the grated ginger. When the aroma of cooked ginger rises, pour in the cooked and cooled dals with the sliced chillies. Stir well to mix. Add the coconut milk and cook for 4-5 minutes. Take off the heat and stir well to blend all the ingredients. Sprinkle over the chopped coriander leaves and cover the pan immediately to save flavours. Serve with warm rice.

Dal with Five Kinds of Vegetables

This is another favourite recipe of the people from Gujarat. As five is an auspicious number for the Hindus, this dish is often cooked as temple food offered to the deity and later shared with the disciples. The authentic vegetables are green plantain, long white radish known as mooli, aubergine, pumpkin and, locally grown snake gourd. I have also used courgette, squash, parsnip, okra and potatoes for this dish.

100g green moong dal
1 tablespoon cooking oil
½ teaspoon fennel seeds
2 bay leaves
100g green plantain, sliced
100g mooli, bite-sized dice
100g aubergines, bite-sized dice smeared with a little salt
and a pinch of ground turmeric
100g pumpkin, bite-sized dice
100g snake gourd or courgette, bite-sized dice
1 teaspoon ground turmeric
1 teaspoon chilli powder
1½ tablespoons ground cumin
1½ tablespoons ground coriander
200g natural yoghurt, beaten
4 tablespoons fine gram flour (besan)
thumb-sized piece root ginger, finely grated
juice of one lemon
1 fresh green or red chilli, sliced
salt, to taste

Boil the dal in approximately 300-400ml water until cooked, and set aside. Heat the oil in a pan and throw in the fennel seeds and bay leaves, then add the vegetables. Stir in the ground turmeric, chilli, cumin and coriander and fry a little before adding just enough water to cover the contents. Next mix the beaten yoghurt with the gram flour and grated ginger and stir in slowly. Cook on a low heat for 10 minutes and add the boiled dal. The art is to blend everything nicely without breaking up the vegetables while cooking.

(cont...)

Be gentle when stirring. This is a creamy dish so maintain the consistency and do not dilute. Take off the heat and add lemon juice and sliced chilli. Serve with rice or plain puri.

Dal Bukhara

Bukhara is a province in Uzbekistan along the old Silk Route to the North West Provinces of undivided India. This ancient recipe was recreated in India recently when it was served to Hilary Clinton on her visit to India in 2009. Slow cooking in a traditional and almost spherical metal bean-pot-like utensil (*handi*) makes this dish distinctive. Most big hotels in India now cook their own version of this, as it's a hit with the tourists.

200g black split urid dal
thumb-sized piece root ginger, grated
6 garlic cloves, crushed
2 tablespoons ghee or clarified butter
4 small cardamom pods
5cm cinnamon stick
6 cloves
2 small tomatoes, peeled and chopped
2 tablespoons thick set yoghurt, beaten
1 tablespoon palm jaggery or brown sugar

Boil the dal in approximately 700ml water with the ginger and garlic till mushy and set aside. Put the ghee or butter in a saucepan and fry the whole garam masala consisting of cardamom pods, cinnamon and cloves. When aromatic, pour the boiled dal into the pan. Stir in the chopped tomatoes. Cook on a low heat for an hour stirring frequently. This is to enable the garam masala to slowly release their flavours into the dal. Keep stirring like you do when you cook a risotto. Make sure that the dal is not burnt at the base of the pan. Stir in the beaten yoghurt with a teaspoon of brown sugar or jaggery and blend well with a whisk. This creamy dal goes well with naan bread and a green crunchy salad.

Moong Dal Laddu

Laddu or laddoo is a traditional Indian sweet ball made with nuts and raisins, grated coconut, sesame seeds or other dals and ghee. According to *The Guinness Book of Records,* the heaviest and largest *laddu* weighed 5,570 kilos! This easy to prepare ceremonial food is popular all over India and is an example of the diverse use of dal as an ingredient. This is also the basic recipe of moong dal halva you can get in a packet from some supermarkets.

400g split yellow moong dal
½ teaspoon ground black cardamom seeds
200g pounded jaggery or brown sugar
3 tablespoons melted ghee or clarified butter

Dry fry the dal till it is light brown and emits a nutty scent. Leave to cool then grind coarsely and add the cardamom seeds and pounded jaggery or brown sugar and mix with warmed ghee or butter. Using your hands swiftly form the mixture into walnut-sized balls. Watch out the mixture does not become too dry to handle. If it does, you can warm it up in a microwave. Laddus can be kept in an airtight container for at least a fortnight and can be warmed a little before serving. Alternatively you can pour the mixture onto a greased plate, cool a little and cut into 3cm cubes and serve as halva pieces.

Spinach with Toor Dal

On a visit to the incredible Jaisalmer fort in western Rajasthan, carved out of gigantic golden sandstone, I had the honour of being invited to a private *haveli* – a traditional house. My Rajput host offered this tasty broth for lunch with handmade unleavened round bread (see page 118). His wife cooked it with mushed toor dal as I watched her.

200g oily toor dal
½ teaspoon ground turmeric
1 tablespoon cooking oil
1 onion, finely sliced
2-3 garlic cloves, crushed garlic
¼ teaspoon mustard seeds
¼ teaspoon cumin seeds
100g whole leaf spinach, fresh or frozen
½ tablespoon ground and roasted gram flour (besan)
1 teaspoon tamarind pulp (mixed in 125ml of warm water)
5 green chillies, cut into small pieces
10-12 curry leaves
1 tablespoon melted ghee or clarified butter
2 dried whole red chillies

Boil the dal in approximately 600ml water with the turmeric until soft, mash into a pulp and set aside. To roast the gram flour, toss it in a hot dry frying pan for 30-40 seconds until a nutty aroma rises. Set aside. Heat the cooking oil in a frying pan with a heavy base. When hot add the sliced onion and brown on a low heat. Throw in the crushed garlic, mustard seeds and the cumin seeds. As they crackle, add the spinach and stir fry with a small sprinkle of the roasted gram flour and a little water.

Pour this over the mushed dal and add the tamarind water, chopped chillies and the curry leaves. Cook for another 3-4 minutes constantly stirring with a hand whisk to blend well. Drizzle the melted ghee over, float the dried whole red chillies on top and take it off the heat. Serve with warm parathas (page 119) or rotis (page 118).

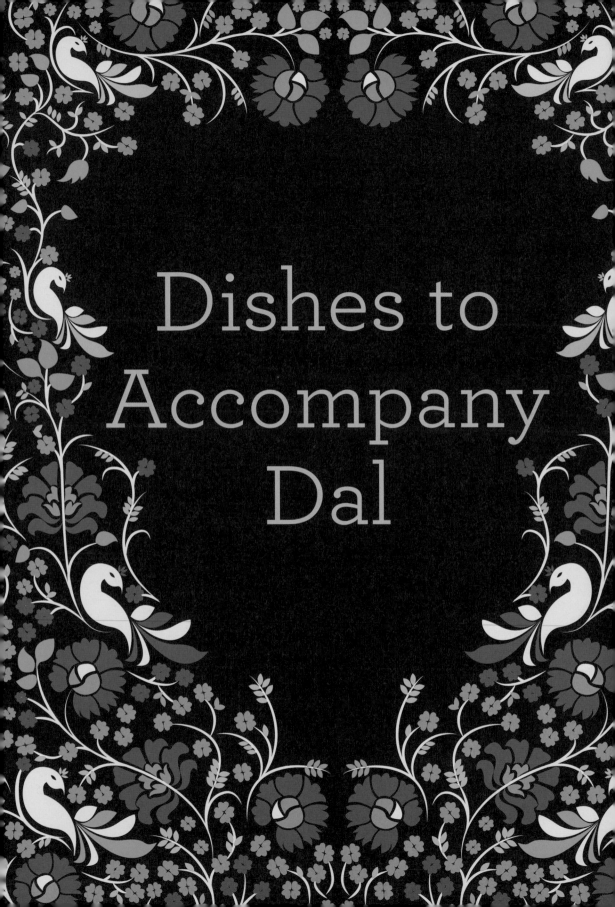

Dishes to Accompany Dal

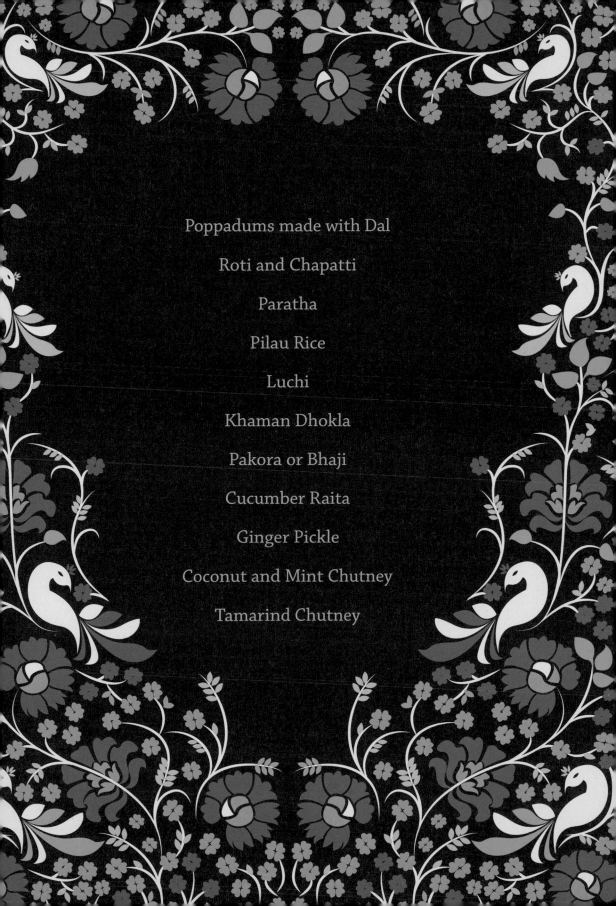

Poppadums made with Dal

Roti and Chapatti

Paratha

Pilau Rice

Luchi

Khaman Dhokla

Pakora or Bhaji

Cucumber Raita

Ginger Pickle

Coconut and Mint Chutney

Tamarind Chutney

Poppadums made with Dal

The humble poppadum invented by the ancient women folk who have been handing down the skills to generations of their daughters, has now become a thriving million-dollar Indian industry. Through a series of precise and deft hand slaps the poppadum makers can transform a mere lump of dal into a tasty edible cracker. This recipe uses a rolling pin and a cutting template. Urid dal flour is available to buy in some shops. If you wish to use moong dal you will need to grind the dal to create flour.

400g urid dal or moong dal flour
¼ teaspoon ground black pepper or crushed dry chillies
¼ teaspoon roughly ground cumin seeds
¼ teaspoon salt

Using all the listed ingredients and sufficient water mix together to make a malleable dough. Divide the dough and turn it into several walnut-sized balls. Smear the work surface lightly with oil and roll out each dough ball into a rough circular shape as thin as possible. Now using an 8-10cm saucer or a suitable metal lid as a template cut them out to perfect circles. If you have a rare hot day in Britain, try to let them dry in the sun on a piece of muslin or on a wire baking rack or (perhaps more realistically!) leave in a switched off warm oven overnight to become crisp. They are now ready to fry, grill or microwave.

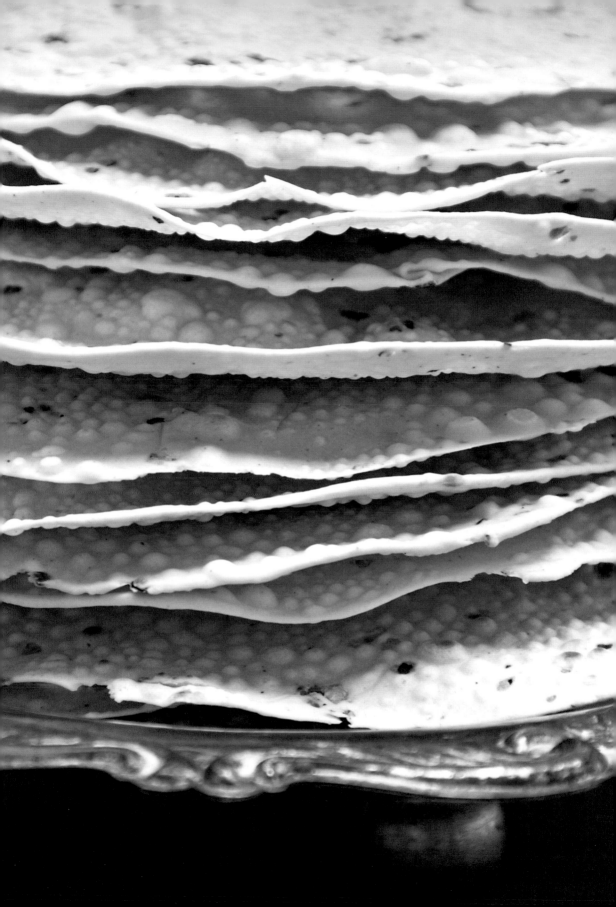

Roti and Chapatti

This is the recipe for basic unleavened dough using high gluten wholemeal *atta* flour.

250g *atta* flour
½ teaspoon cooking oil
150ml tepid water
1 tablespoon ghee
salt, to taste

Place the *atta* in a bowl (saving a little flour to dust the rolling board later) with the cooking oil and a pinch of salt. Gradually add the water a few drops at a time and knead the mixture until it becomes a soft and malleable dough. Take your time kneading (10-15 minutes). The longer you knead the softer the roti will be. Once the dough is prepared, set aside at room temperature to stand for 10 minutes.

Now divide the dough into 6-8 ping pong ball-sized pieces and roll them into spheres.

Dust the surface with flour. Using a rolling pin roll out each ball into discs approximately 15cm in diameter.

Heat an Indian *tawa* or a heavy frying pan well and place one disc on it. Leave it to cook for 1 minute. Pat and press it down all over with a wooden spatula for another 30 seconds until you see small bubbles appear on the surface. Turn it over and repeat the process on the other side. By then you should smell cooked bread. Once evenly browned on both sides, it is ready to serve.

When you brush the roti with ghee or fry on the *tawa* with a teaspoon of ghee, it becomes a chapatti but plain roti only has ghee in the dough.

Paratha

The word *parat* means layer in Hindi. Paratha is a pan-fried layered unleavened flat bread originating from Punjab. This basic recipe can be adapted with various meat or vegetable fillings between the layers. It is a good accompaniment for thicker varieties of rich north Indian dals.

250g *atta* flour
½ teaspoon cooking oil
150ml tepid water
4-6 tablespoons ghee
salt, to taste

Place the *atta* in a bowl (saving a little flour to dust the rolling board later) with half a teaspoon of cooking oil and a pinch of salt. Gradually add the water a few drops at a time and knead the mixture until it becomes a soft and malleable dough. Take your time kneading (10-15 minutes). The longer you knead the softer the paratha will be. Once the dough is prepared, set aside at room temperature to stand for 10 minutes.

Now divide the dough into 6-8 ping pong ball-sized pieces and roll them into spheres.

Dust the surface with dry flour. Using a rolling pin roll out each ball into discs approximately 15-16cm in diameter.

Smear the disc all over with a teaspoon of ghee using your fingers. Fold it in half. Smear the semi circle with ½ teaspoon of ghee and fold it in half again so you are left with a quarter. Dust the surface again with flour and roll it. The shape will resemble a triangle measuring approximately 15cm on two sides with a slightly curved third side.

Heat a teaspoon of ghee in an Indian *tawa* or a heavy frying pan and place the triangle on it. Leave it to cook for 1 minute. Pat and press all over it with a wooden spatula for another 30 seconds to see the small bubbles appear. Turn it over and add one more teaspoon of ghee over the other side. Pat and press on the other side. The greased layers of the fold should by now achieve a crispy puff pastry-like texture. When the brown spots begin to appear on the surface and you can smell the fried bread, take off the heat and stack them in a suitable container to keep warm ready to serve.

Pilau Rice

The word pilau or pullau came from Persia meaning a rice cuisine, via the Turkish Pilav to the Spanish Paella and transformed into Pilau in India. It is basically plain rice cooked by gradual absorption of water and flavoured with ghee and various combinations of spices. This is the basic recipe.

250g basmati rice
450ml boiling water
1 tablespoon ghee
5cm piece cinnamon
6 green cardamom pods
6 cloves

Rinse the rice with cold water and leave it aside for 10 minutes. Use a lidded saucepan to heat the ghee first. When hot throw in the cinnamon, cardamom and cloves and fry for 30 seconds, then add the washed rice and fry for another 30 seconds. Add the boiling water and wait for it to bubble. As soon as it starts to bubble, reduce the heat by half and cover the pan. Cook for 6-7 minutes for the rice to absorb the water. Now turn the heat down to the minimum and let it cook for another 6-7 minutes and turn the heat off. Leave it there for 5-6 minutes and then check for the dryness and to see if it has cooked to your requirement. Pick a couple of cooked grains with a spoon and bite. If you need you may have to sprinkle a little warm water at this stage and leave it lidded in a warm place without the heat like a switched off warm oven. Fluff it up with a fork before serving.

Luchi

Luchi is a doughnut-sized, deep-fried puffed-up bread from Bengal, mostly made with white flour. A north Indian wholemeal version of this is known as puri. You need a *karahi* or a wok for deep-frying. A shallow frying pan is unsuitable. Ideally for aesthetic reasons, luchi should be eaten freshly fried from the *karahi* puffed up not as deflated discs. However very few people these days can manage to fry and serve them quickly enough for them to stay puffed. Luckily flat luchis taste just as good.

400g refined white flour
2 teaspoons ghee
200ml water, approximately
150ml melted ghee, approximately

Place the flour in a bowl (saving a little flour to dust the rolling board later) with the 2 teaspoons of ghee. Gradually add water a few drops at a time and knead the mixture until it becomes a soft and malleable dough. Take your time kneading (10–15 minutes). The longer you knead the puffier the luchis will be. Once the dough is prepared, set aside at room temperature to stand for 10 minutes.

Now divide the dough into 6-8 walnut-sized pieces and roll them into spheres. Flatten them slightly between the palms and set aside.

Dust the surface with dry flour. Using a rolling pin roll out each ball into a circle approximately 8–10cm in diameter. Try and roll them as close to perfect circles as you can. Now heat the ghee in your *karahi* and turn down the temperature just before frying the luchi. Deep fry each disc in the hot ghee. The moisture in the dough makes it puff out almost instantly – each luchi should take no longer than 20 seconds. The amount of ghee will depend on the size of your *karahi* and you may need more. There is also a technique of placing the rolled out luchi into the hot ghee safely without splashing. You need to lower it very gently – almost like floating a devotional offering in the river Ganges. It takes practice. As soon as the luchi puffs up and turns into light beige in colour you take it out using a stainless steel perforated skimmer and serve.

Khaman Dhokla

Khaman dhokla is a steam-baked savoury cake made from fermented dal batter and yoghurt. Different varieties of dhokla can be made with other combinations of ingredients such as ground rice, urid dal or chana dal. Originating from Gujarat, this preparation has travelled all over India and abroad and gained popularity as a tasty wholesome vegetarian snack. This simple recipe uses gram flour and no rice.

300g gram flour (besan)
200g natural yoghurt, beaten
2 tablespoons cooking oil
½ teaspoon bicarbonate soda
thumb-sized piece fresh ginger, grated
½ teaspoon chilli powder
½ teaspoon ground turmeric
salt, to taste

For tempering
2 tablespoons cooking oil
1 teaspoon mustard seeds
3-4 curry leaves
pinch of asafoetida (*hing*)
1 tablespoon coriander leaves, chopped
2 green chillies, vertically slit

Mix the gram flour with the beaten yoghurt, oil, bicarbonate soda, and little water in a bowl to make into a smooth and thick batter. Cover the batter with a tea towel and set aside at room temperature for 4 hours to ferment.

Now add the ginger, chilli and turmeric to the batter and blend well. Pour the mixture into a lidded pudding basin and steam in a pan of water on high heat for 10–15 minutes. Allow it to cool then cut into approximately 5cm cubes and lay them on a dish.

Put the 2 tablespoons of oil in a frying pan. When hot throw in the mustard seeds, curry leaves and asafoetida. As the seeds crackle, take the pan off the heat and pour over the dhokla pieces.

Garnish with chopped coriander and green chillies. Serve with coconut and mint chutney (page 128).

Pakora or Bhaji

Pakoras or bhajis are pieces of raw vegetables such as potatoes, onions, aubergines, and cauliflower coated in a spiced gram flour batter and deep fried. Bhajis use shredded vegetables whereas pakoras use whole or sliced vegetables. Both are pan-Indian cheap, popular and tasty street savouries.

225g whole or sliced pieces of vegetable of choice such as cauliflower florets, whole mushrooms, sliced aubergines or paneer pieces (if you are making pakoras)

or

225g washed and thinly shredded vegetable of choice such as potatoes, cabbage and onions (if you are making bhajis)
100ml to 200ml vegetable oil for deep frying (amount varies with the size of *karahi* or wok)

For the batter
100g gram flour (besan)
1 teaspoon ground cumin
1 teaspoon ground coriander
½ teaspoon chilli powder
1 tablespoon ground masoor dal
½ teaspoon fenugreek seeds (*methi*)
salt, to taste

Mix the batter ingredients together well with enough water to make a thick paste that can easily stick to the vegetables and stay on as coating.

For making pakoras: Heat the oil to a chip frying temperature. Coat the vegetable pieces one at a time in the batter and put carefully straight into the hot oil in a batch of 3-4 at a time and fry for about 2-3 minutes, drain on a piece of kitchen towel and keep warm. Lay them on a plate and serve with pickles, chutney or dips.

For making bhajis: Use the same batter ingredients and make a thick paste with water. Now mix the shredded vegetables with it so that it becomes one whole lumpy and glutinous batter. Put one tablespoon of batter and

(cont...)

vegetable mix carefully straight into the hot oil for one bhaji in batches of 3-4 at a time and fry for about 2-3 minutes, drain on a piece of kitchen towel and keep warm. Lay them on a plate and serve with pickles, chutney or dips like the pakoras.

Cucumber Raita

½ cucumber
200g natural yoghurt
¼ teaspoon chilli powder
¼ teaspoon ground cumin
juice from ½ lemon
salt, to taste

Slice the cucumber in 2cm thick circular pieces. Cut each piece lengthwise into matchsticks. Beat the yoghurt and mix the cucumber pieces well with chilli, cumin, lemon juice and salt. Keep it in the fridge for 4 hours before serving. It will keep for a week in your fridge but cannot be frozen.

Ginger Pickle

2 pieces of fresh root ginger (5-6cm long)
200ml white wine vinegar
50ml good quality mustard oil
1 tablespoon white mustard seeds
½ tablespoon roasted coriander seeds
10 garlic cloves, peeled and sliced
2 thinly sliced chillies – one red and one green
salt, to taste

Peel and slice the fresh ginger into 1.5cm long pieces, then cut each piece lengthwise into matchsticks.

Put all the ingredients in a glass jar with plastic (non-metallic) airtight lid. Shake vigorously for 3-5 minutes. Leave in a cool dark place and shake at least once daily for a week. It is now ready to use and will keep for a fortnight in the fridge.

Coconut and Mint Chutney

125g grated coconut, fresh, creamed or desiccated soaked in milk
125g coarsely chopped mint leaves
juice from 1 lemon
2 fresh green chillies, whole
½ teaspoon sugar
salt, to taste

Whizz the ingredients in a blender for a minute or two. Pour the mixture into a glass jar with a non-metalic lid and place in the fridge. The chutney will keep for a couple of days.

Tamarind Chutney

100g tamarind puree
50g pitted dates
50g brown sugar
½ teaspoon chilli powder or 1 teaspoon chilli sauce
thumb-sized piece fresh ginger, grated
1 teaspoon powdered garam masala
salt, to taste

Blend the ingredients in a food processor, adding just enough water to make a dip. Put in a bowl and serve. You can keep it in the fridge in a non-metallic lidded glass container for a week.

GLOSSARY OF INDIAN TERMS

BESAN   Unlike *sattu* – a mixture of toasted lentils and cereals – besan is flour made from chickpeas or channa (gram) dal. It is high in carbohydrate but contains no gluten.

CHEVDA   Fried spicy snacks made with gram flour.

GATHIA   A variety of fried snack like the *Chevda*.

GARAM MASALA   The Hindi word literally means 'hot or heat inducing spices' composed of cardamom pods, cloves, cinnamon bark with other regionally preferred seeds like cumin. The whole spices are toasted first then ground. Often fried whole spices are used for slow cooking. Garam masala you see in supermarkets should be used promptly otherwise they will lose flavour. I dry toast the whole ones and grind them in a pestle and mortar.

GRAM   A smaller, darker, and regional variety of chickpeas. Also known as Bengal gram or black gram (*kala chana*).

HAVELI   Western Indian houses elaborately decorated with fine carving and portraits and legends painted on the walls.

HALVA Etymologically the word has Arabic origin meaning sweet confection made from vegetables, fruits, nuts and lentils with fat and sugar.

HANDI The word originally means the ancient form of clay pot designed for slow cooking. Like the American bean pot it has a bulging body with a narrow round opening with a separate lid. Food cooked in this vessel is often named after the pot to signify the dish. For example, there is a well-known dish called Handi Biriyani.

HING Pan Indian name for asafoetida. See recipes for details.

JAGGERY The traditional unrefined sugar made from sugar cane or date palm, much consumed in India as a cheaper and better alternative to sugar. It has some religious significance to the Hindus as a celebratory and holy food.

KARAHI Cooking pot with two loop handles on either sides and rounded bottom almost like a Chinese wok but deeper, used for stir-frying and to prepare pappy food.

LUCHI Deep-fried circular puffed bread roughly 10-12cm in diameter, also known as puri, made with white or wholemeal flour – a delicacy in Bengal, Assam and Orissa. It is usually deep fried in a *karahi* in clarified butter or ghee.

NAAN The Indian oven-cooked flatbread leavened with yeast and yoghurt and served brushed in ghee or clarified butter.

PANCH PHORAN The word in Bengali literally means a mixture of five spices. These are black mustard seeds, cumin seeds, fenugreek seeds, nigella seeds and fennel seeds. These are always fried together whole and not ground, to release flavours for tempering.

PANEER Ancient form of homemade cheese widely used in India as meat substitute for vegetarians. It is now widely available.

PARATHA   Shallow-fried unleavened flatbread that can be circular, square or triangular shaped and can be stuffed with pastes of dals, gram flour or vegetables.

PILAU RICE   The word, migrated into other languages in different forms, has a Persian origin. In India the rice is first fried in ample ghee and then cooked in a gravy of spices including garam masala and saffron with or without meat and vegetables.

RAITA   The Indian yoghurt dip made with ground cumin, chilli, and salt, often with finely sliced or pulverised onions and cucumber, chopped mint and coriander leaves added in the mix. It is meant to cool the palate from the heat of spicy food. Some raitas contain pea-sized fried chickpea and dal batter balls, now available in Asian grocers.

ROTI   Most common variety of circular Indian flat bread made with durum wheat flour also known as *atta*. Rotis are not fried but cooked on a shallow slightly conclave iron griddle with a handle and open flame.

FURTHER READING

Monsoon Diary by Shoba Narayan, Bantam Books

Curry by Lizzie Collingham, Vintage Books

The Bean Book by Rose Elliot, Thorsons

Life and Food In Bengal by Chitrita Banerji, Weidenfeld & Nicolson

INDEX

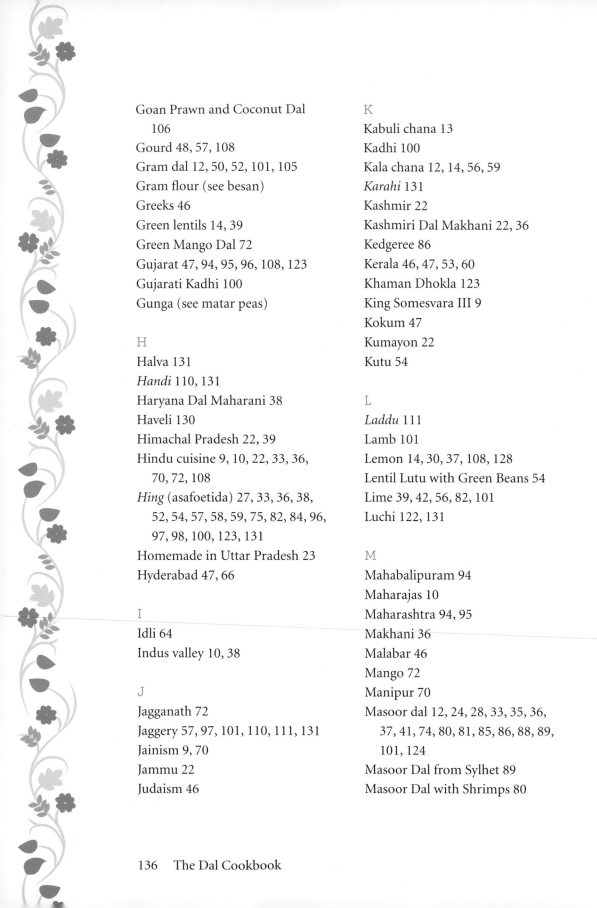

ACKNOWLEDGEMENTS

One ordinary afternoon in 2010 as I was cooking dal for the evening meal, I heard a BBC Radio 4 programme on food writing interviewing my publisher-to-be Anne Dolamore. As I listened the idea of proffering her a book proposal on dal germinated in my mind. After some solitary deliberation I sent my idea to her and went away to India partly to visit the family and partly in search of more dal recipes. After sometime, when I had almost resigned myself to a rejection, Anne's letter expressing interest in the project arrived. In response I emailed her some of the work I had done on the subject, and to my delight, she asked to read the rest.

Thank you Anne for your faith in my work and publishing the book.

My friend Ariadne Van de Ven for always lending me her ears. Thank you for all those stimulating discussions on the topic over bowls full of dals. Thanks also to Jenny Clark, another good friend, who read the first few draft recipes and made some useful suggestions. I am also grateful to Shanthi Sivanesan who helped me with the translation of some Tamil words. And of course, my daughter Ronita who was very keen that I should write down the recipes for her, her offspring and the diaspora at large. Thanks for the encouragement my love.

Very special heartfelt thanks to Nancy Campbell who read through the entire text and made some valuable changes and suggestions. I was touched by your enormous generosity and kindness. You have earned yourself and your family a lifetime supply of my various dals.

I am also indebted to the numerous Indian cooks and food enthusiasts who shared their local knowledge and expertise with me. Finally I thank those friends and guests who tasted my dal cooking and delighted me with their appreciation.

NOTES

NOTES